# CHOICES
## AT THE
# HEART
## OF
# TECHNOLOGY

## A CHRISTIAN PERSPECTIVE

# Christian Mission and Modern Culture

EDITED BY
ALAN NEELY, H. WAYNE PIPKIN,
AND WILBERT R. SHENK

In the Series:

*Believing in the Future*, by David J. Bosch

*Write the Vision*, by Wilbert R. Shenk

*Truth and Authority in Modernity*,
by Lesslie Newbigin

*Religion and the Variety of Culture*,
by Lamin Sanneh

*The End of Christendom and the Future of Christianity*,
by Douglas John Hall

*The Mission of Theology and Theology as Mission*,
by J. Andrew Kirk

*The Missionary Congregation, Leadership, and Liminality*,
by Alan J. Roxburgh

*A Spacious Heart*,
by Judith M. Gundry-Volf and Miroslav Volf

*The Secular Experience of God*,
by Kenneth Cragg

*Secularization and Mission*,
by Bert Hoedemaker

*Living Faithfully in a Fragmented World,*
by Jonathan R. Wilson

*Into the Vacuum: Being the Church
in the Age of Barbarism,*
by Gordon Scoville

*Speaking the Truth in Love,*
by James V. Brownson

*From Complicity to Encounter,*
by Jane Collier and Rafael Esteban

*Canon and Mission,*
by H. D. Beeby

*Missiological Implications of Epistemological Shifts,*
by Paul G. Hiebert

*Liberating Evangelism,*
by Stephen L. Pickard

*Beyond Sectarianism,*
by Philip D. Kenneson

*Another City,*
by Barry Harvey

*Choices at the Heart of Technology,*
by Ruth Conway

*The Change of Conversion and the Origin of Christendom,*
by Alan Kreider

*Power, Truth, and Community in Modern Culture,*
by Charles C. West

# CHOICES
## AT THE
# HEART
## OF
# TECHNOLOGY

## A CHRISTIAN PERSPECTIVE

# RUTH CONWAY

TRINITY PRESS
INTERNATIONAL
HARRISBURG, PENNSYLVANIA

Trinity Press International, P.O. Box 1321, Harrisburg, PA 17105

Trinity Press International is a division of The Morehouse Group.

Copyright © 1999 Ruth Conway

Unless otherwise noted, Scripture quotations are from *The Revised English Bible*, Oxford and Cambridge University Presses, 1989, and are used by permission.

Cover design: Brian Preuss

**Library of Congress Cataloging-in-Publication Data**
Conway, Ruth.
    Choices at the heart of technology : a Christian perspective / Ruth Conway.
        p. cm. — (Christian mission and modern culture)
    Includes bibliographical references.
    ISBN 1-56338-287-3   (pbk. : alk. paper)
    1. Technology—Religious aspects—Christianity.
I. Title. II. Series.
  BR115.T42 C66    1999
  261.5'6 21—dc21

                                    99–045070
                                    CIP

*Printed in the United States of America*
99  00  01  02  03  04  6  5  4  3  2  1

# Contents

PREFACE TO THE SERIES                                      ix

ACKNOWLEDGMENTS                                            xi

1. DISCERNING THE POWERS OF TECHNOLOGY                      1

PART A: HIDDEN MESSAGES

2. NAMING THE POWERS OF TECHNOLOGY                          7

3. WORLDVIEWS GOVERNING TECHNOLOGY                         27

PART B: INSIGHTS FROM BIBLICAL FAITH

4. DREAMS AND DELUSIONS OF DEVELOPMENT                     37

5. NURTURE AND COMPASSION                                  49

6. LETTING GO OF CONTROL: FREEDOM FOR THE OTHER            57

7. JUST RELATIONSHIPS                                      71

8. COMMUNICATION THAT MATTERS                              87

9. LEARNING IN AND FOR COMMUNITY                          101

10. A CONCLUDING INVITATION                               113

NOTES                                                     117

REFERENCES CITED                                          119

# Preface to the Series

Both Christian mission and modern culture, widely regarded as antagonists, are in crisis. The emergence of the modern mission movement in the early nineteenth century cannot be understood apart from the rise of technocratic society. Now, at the end of the twentieth century, both modern culture and Christian mission face an uncertain future.

One of the developments integral to modernity was the way the role of religion in culture was redefined. Whereas religion had played an authoritative role in the culture of Christendom, modern culture was highly critical of religion and increasingly secular in its assumptions. A sustained effort was made to banish religion to the backwaters of modern culture.

The decade of the 1980s witnessed further momentous developments on the geopolitical front with the collapse of communism. In the aftermath of the breakup of the system of power blocs that dominated international relations for a generation, it is clear that religion has survived even if its institutionalization has undergone deep change and its future forms are unclear. Secularism continues to oppose religion, while technology has emerged as a major source of power and authority in modern culture. Both confront Christian faith with fundamental questions.

The purpose of this series is to probe these developments from a variety of angles with a view to helping the church understand its missional responsibility to a culture in crisis. One important resource is the church's experience of two centuries of cross-cultural mission that has reshaped the church into a global Christian *ecumene.* The focus of our inquiry will be the church in modern culture. The series (1) examines modern/postmodern culture from a missional point of view; (2) develops the theological agenda that the church in modern culture must address in order to recover its own integrity; and (3) tests fresh conceptualizations of the nature and mission of the church as it engages modern culture. In other words, these volumes are intended to be a forum where conventional assumptions can be challenged and alternative formulations explored.

This series is a project authorized by the Institute of Mennonite Studies, research agency of the Associated Mennonite Biblical Seminary, and supported by a generous grant from the Pew Charitable Trusts.

# Acknowledgments

---

The writing of this book, which has come about only by the prompting and patience of Wilbert Shenk, has brought together two areas of my experience. On the one hand, I have been working alongside design and technology teachers, teacher educators, and curriculum developers at a time when technology education is being established as a vital school subject in many countries. The VALIDATE network (see Note 2) has been especially formative and fruitful. On the other hand, I have been stimulated, not least by Lesslie Newbigin's insights and "The Gospel and Our Culture" studies, to reflect with other Christians on the part that technology plays in today's dominant global culture. I owe a great deal to colleagues and friends from both these circles for all they have taught me, particularly those who were willing to read the first draft and make critical comments. Among the "technology" colleagues, I must mention David Layton as the one who has promoted the inclusion of "values issues" in technology curricula worldwide and who initially brought me into the debate, and John Olson and Denis Stewart, who gave valuable time to read the draft. Among the "theological reflectors" to whom I owe a direct debt are Donald Eadie, Peter Fulljames, Pat Page, David Stevens, Brent Waters, and, above all, my husband, Martin. Anne Riggs deserves a special mention both for her friendship and for her creative participation with me in both circles. I have, of course, been greatly dependent on those who have studied aspects of the nature and influence of technology in far greater depth than I ever could and who have provided thought-provoking analyses. I have drawn on their work extensively. I am grateful to all who have opened doors to enable this learning experience and who have encouraged me to take it further. I alone remain entirely responsible for the understanding I have then tried to express.

# 1

# Discerning the Powers of Technology

## A Mixed Blessing?

Modern technology, informed by an ever-deeper pene-
tration of nature and propelled by the forces of market
and politics, has enhanced human power beyond anything known or even dreamed of before.... But the
other side of the triumphal advance has begun to show
its face, disturbing the euphoria of success with
threats that are as novel as its welcomed fruits. Not
counting the insanity of a sudden, suicidal atomic
holocaust,... it is the peaceful and constructive use of
worldwide technological power, a use in which all of us
collaborate as captive beneficiaries through rising production, consumption, and sheer population growth,
that poses threats much harder to counter. The net
total of these threats is the overtaxing of nature,
[both] environmental and (perhaps) human (Jonas
1984:ix).

There are technical solutions to eco-social problems.
They must be vigorously pursued. We will need all the
earth-friendly technologies we can muster. At the
same time, and several planes deeper, appropriate
technology may not even be conceived, much less

pursued, if reigning worldviews (or "cosmologies") are haywire. Technologies express cultures. Ways of doing things reflect ways of seeing things (Rasmussen 1996:181).

Tools are concrete commitments to certain ways of doing things, and therefore certain ways of dividing power (Pursell 1994:218).

Within a few short centuries we human beings have transformed the face of the earth, laying hold of the resources of the planet and constructing environments matched to the perceived needs and aspirations of human communities: every city bears witness to the ingenuity of human design; every hospital to human techniques for saving and prolonging life; every TV screen and computer monitor to the information and communication networks with which we have circled the earth; every supermarket and fashion store to the successful creation of global markets; every highway and airport terminal to the engineering of vastly increased mobility. But there is another side to the experience from which no one can be completely isolated. To a greater or lesser degree, people are aware of clouds of smog blanketing the cities; of rising sea levels threatening island and coastal dwellers; of land degraded, deforestation, reduced biodiversity, and small-scale farmers forced into poverty by the methods employed by multinational agribusinesses; of the lack of contact and partnership as we stare at VDUs and TV screens; of the widening gap between the haves and have-nots; of the terrifying trade in arms worldwide; of the unresolved (and unresolvable?) problems of nuclear waste.

We are part of a world frantically pushing at technological frontiers, fascinated by the wonders of human ingenuity, seized by the potential for ever-increasing "value-added" goods, dependent on systems of organization that overcome frustrations of distance, time, and complexity. At the same time, we are also part of a world whose technologies are threatening the very basis of life, leading to scarce and poisoned water, infertile soil, polluted air, and a shattering of the relationships that nurture a sense of belonging and companionship. The human species, the apparent flowering of the slow, precarious evolution of life on this planet, seems set on destroying its life-giving arteries. To change the metaphor, with the help of state-of-the-art technology, human beings are cutting off the branch of the tree of life on which all living things sit. Having honed the techniques of planning, management, and control, human beings are apparently incapable of changing a global course that now seems both unpredictable and unmanageable.

How do you and I, individuals within specific human communities, try to understand the cultural tide that is sweeping us along, palpably enhancing lifestyles and expectations for some while leaving all too many floundering in confusion and poverty? Given the resources, ability, creativity, and sensitivity with which humans are endowed, how have we arrived at this critical state, both exhilarating and desperate at the same time?

## A Crisis of Culture

These are not questions that are primarily about the treatment of "the environment," asking how development could be made more sustainable and earth's resources managed more efficiently. They point to a crisis of culture:

> The crisis is that a now-globalizing culture *in* nature and wholly *of* nature runs full grain *against* it. A virile, comprehensive way of life is destructive of nature and human community together—this is the crisis. Soils, peoples, air, and water are being depleted and degraded together. (Or, on our better days, are being sustained together.) It is not "the environment" that is unsustainable. It is a much more inclusive reality, something like life-as-we-have-come-to-know-it.... Life-as-we-have-come-to-know-it is eating itself alive. Modernity devours its own children (Rasmussen 1996:7).

This all-enveloping culture is a technological one. Human beings, gifted with consciousness and vision, have not been content to live within the rhythms and boundaries that are suggested by our place and part in nature; rather, we have seized the initiative to create our own conditions for living. We are surrounded by what we ourselves have made, from do-it-yourself toys and tools to the processes and products of manufacturing industry, from wind-powered irrigation pumps to nuclear power plants, from tractors to airplanes, from garden spades to mining equipment, from wheelchairs to missiles, from telephones to networked computers, from disposable diapers to sewage systems. We inhabit a constructed culture, bent to human-centered desires and goals. This shaping is so strong that it feels as if we are in the grip of a technological power that is out of control. We are tempted simply to battle for a place on the topside of the advance and steer clear of the underside. But that would be to abdicate responsibility precisely when responsible thought and action are most needed. The power needs to be "named" and "engaged" (see Wink's definitive books: *Naming the Powers* 1984, *Unmasking the Powers* 1986, *Engaging the Powers* 1992).

## Probing the Process

To name the powers there must first be an understanding of how technologies, in all their immense variety, are developed, promoted, evaluated, and then incorporated into our lives and culture(s). What decisions are made and by whom? Who is consulted and how? What value judgments are made and with what criteria and timescales? What are the dominant motives? Where are the sources of inspiration? How are the skills acquired? Who orders the priorities, and what sets the pace? What infrastructures are both needed and affected? How does each particular technology interact with people's lives, the fabric of society, and the earth's delicately balanced ecosystems? These are the questions that probe the process by which the power steals in on us, without jolting our attention or setting off the warning signals. They are also the questions customarily avoided:

> Individual habits, perceptions, concepts of self, ideas of space and time, social relationships, and moral and

political boundaries have all been powerfully restructured in the course of modern technological development.... But we are seldom inclined to examine, discuss, or judge pending innovations with broad, keen awareness of what those changes mean. In the technical realm we repeatedly enter into a series of social contracts, the terms of which are revealed only after the signing (Winner 1986:9).

Or as Neil Postman puts it: "Technology redefines 'freedom,' 'truth,' 'intelligence,' 'fact,' 'wisdom,' 'memory,' 'history'—all the words we live by. And it does not pause to tell us. And we do not pause to ask" (1993:8).

Naming must unmask the way in which technology itself manages to divert the attention of its creators and undermine the proper responsibilities they should be shouldering for the care of life-as-we-have-come-to-know-it. We need to discern how the direction is often unwittingly being set and consolidated. This I attempt in the chapter on naming the powers of technology (Chapter 2). That is followed by a chapter that looks behind the decision making and the procedures to the chosen maps: the worldviews and defining purposes. It is these frames of reference that lie at the heart of the shaping of the technological culture. In the end it is these that need questioning most sharply.

Those of us who are Christians come to this task with beliefs that do not readily engage with the most prevalent worldviews within Western technological culture.

Why is that? Because it is a culture which has been immensely successful in developing powerful modes of explaining, understanding and acting in the world which are based on the world's independence from anything external to it. The frames of reference we habitually employ as we analyse, interpret, communicate, judge, and act in our public lives and work exclude any reference to God (McFadyen 1997:60).

It is assumed that God and the world of technological decision making are unrelated. The challenge for Christians, therefore, is to root their critique in the fundamental affirmation "that the trinitarian God is intimately and dynamically present in, active in, and related to the world" (:62), thus resetting technological activity in the context of God's creative and saving action. In the second part of this book I try to suggest how faith in God, who is not only the Creator but also the Redeemer and the Sustainer of the creation in its intradependent wholeness (that is, in all its internal dynamic relationships), offers the possibility of a radical engagement with the powers of technology and ultimately the hope of transformation.

# Part A:
# Hidden Messages

# 2

# Naming the Powers of Technology

### All the More Power Because of Blinkers

The race to extend human experience and capabilities can be likened to a horse race: the going is faster when the horses wear blinkers. Many of the dazzling successes of technology are due to what has been omitted. There are at least five ways in which this takes place.

First, in the development of a technology, the goals, more often than not, relate to performance, efficiency, return on investment, market potential, trendiness. Blinkers are in place when it comes to assessing the effect on the quality of life of the people touched, be they users or those involved in the development, manufacture, marketing, or eventual disposal. Little notice is taken of the likely impact on employment patterns and structures of community, on relationships that affirm identity and belonging, on experiences that carry symbolic meaning for people, on long-term health, and on the environment. All these are typically left out of count as "externalities." We should then hardly be surprised that the technology is experienced as a power that is *insensitive* to what has been deliberately omitted. Langdon Winner cites dozens of sophisticated energy studies conducted during the 1970s in response to what was then called "the energy crisis." But in the end, efficiency was the sole criterion:

"Regardless of how a particular energy solution would affect the distribution of wealth and social power, the case for or against it had to be stated as practical necessity deriving from demonstrable conditions of technical or economic efficiency" (1986:53).

There is a parallel in the question posed in Michael Christie's article "Aboriginal Science for the Ecologically Sustainable Future": "How can you expect science to solve your human problems if it depends on an ontology which accords things their scientific value only after they have been abstracted from the day to day social and political and economic context?" (1991:28).

Second, the reference to science is not coincidental: many technologies are science based and share the same assumptions of objectivity and rationality. Both science and technology run the danger of becoming ideologies that impose their own form of reasoning and rule following to the exclusion of personal values and a wider sense of purpose. Technologies are often designed so as to leave no room for situational human judgments that might divert or subvert the smooth running of the preplanned program: "Rather than encouraging personal autonomy, creativity, and moral responsibility, many jobs and machines are designed to eliminate these qualities altogether" (Winner 1992:56). Ursula Franklin has commented: "People are seen as sources of problems while technology is seen as a source of solutions" (1992:76). This turns the technology into a *marginalizing* power: "The notion that maybe technology constitutes a source of problems and grievances and people might be looked upon as a source of solutions has very rarely entered public policy or even public consciousness" (:76). This was forcefully illustrated in 1992 when the London Ambulance Service put into operation a £1.5 million newly computerized system to handle calls for its three hundred emergency ambulances:

> It took just 36 hours of full operation for the system to collapse…. Many LAS staff found the new system to be

an operational straitjacket; their attempts to continue operating local flexibility were at loggerheads with the rigidity of the system.... Changes to the layout of the control-room meant that staff were working in unfamiliar positions, without paper backup, and were less able to work with colleagues with whom they had jointly solved problems before.

Factors that should have been integrated into the design include operators giving drivers five minutes for a smoke or allowing emergency calls to be switched between vehicles when the need arose rather than on the basis of predefined allocation figures and statistical analysis. Because the system failed to take account of these and many other human elements, it rapidly became unworkable (Patel 1993).

The scale and nature of the corporate organization around a technological endeavor, particularly the fragmentation of work, are often what conspire to undermine any feeling of personal responsibility for the overall purpose or impact. "Engineers in modern technological society have come to be hired by organizations... and are able to enjoy his or her life without any consciousness of the specified end user of the technology (or of its influence on all citizens and the natural environment)" (Furuya 1989:2). Or again, "it is hard to find anyone who admits to making nuclear bombs or designing cruise missiles. All anyone ever designs are gears or devices" (Franklin 1985:17).

Third, there is one particularly damaging aspect of this omission of personal value judgments and sense of responsibility: the deliberate attempt to reduce the influence of ethical considerations about what *ought* to be done in favor of what *can* be done. This is seen starkly in the field of genetic engineering, where the push to develop and use techniques of genetic manipulation has joined forces with the vested interests of the food and pharmaceutical industries. Inadequate discussion of the moral issues is enshrined in the patenting laws that now govern the development and use of these technologies. Those laws give rights of ownership and control to transnational corporations producing profit-making products for the global market. There are disturbing consequences: widespread "biopiracy," including human gene prospecting and a trade in indigenous DNA; third-world farmers forced into bankruptcy by having to "buy back" genetically modified seed; the likelihood of the appearance of antibiotic-resistant diseases and unpredictable allergies; massive increases in pesticide use and severe reduction in the diversity of crops (which both carry their own dire consequences); funds being channeled into what is commercially profitable rather than into the public good. The decisions concerning the priorities in biotechnological research and development, combined with a legislative framework geared to market interests, are creating *immoral* powers.

Weapons production is another obvious and alarming example: the process of designing and constructing nuclear fighting systems both needs and produces an effective mechanism of dissociation between the personal responsibility of those involved in production and the eventual outcomes of their work. Furthermore, "weapons can be perceived as desirable within a system which makes the market the arbiter of value; a product is sanctified by being sold" (Barnett 1994:59). The arms trade is a terrifying witness to a technology disengaged from ethical considerations.

Fourth, technologies also share the "sins of omission" of the economic systems with which they are in symbiotic relationship—because money is invested in their development and they in turn provide return on that investment. The global economic system is demonstrably one of the root causes of the crisis being experienced in nature. Herman Daly has argued that "the macroeconomy is seen as an isolated system (i.e., involving no exchanges of matter or energy with its environment) in which exchange-value circulates between firms and households in a closed loop" (Daly 1993:40). No account is taken, therefore, of the macroeconomy's dependence on nature: on nature's limited resources, on its adaptability to change, and on its capacity to absorb the polluting wastes of our technological activities. If no account is taken in the financial boardrooms, then no account will be taken by designers, engineers, and manufacturers when they decide on materials, energy supplies, production sites, and waste disposal. No wonder we are in the grip of a *destructive* power that is causing irreversible damage to nature's life-sustaining processes!

Fifth, technological powers have been strongly shaped by the omission of the experience and perspectives of women. The effects of this marginalization have been summarized by Patricia Hynes, Director of the Institute on Women and Technology, Amherst, Massachusetts, in her Introduction to *Reconstructing Babylon*:

> Women have never lived without technology. Yet we have barely a toehold in the discourse and direction of it....

> Asked, on the eve of World War II, how we are to prevent war, Virginia Woolf replied that developing and using weapons in war and in hunt "has always been the man's habit, not the woman's."...

> After World War II, the politicians of agribusiness and the chemical industry built their defense of the new pesticide-based agriculture on the metaphor of war, with insects as enemies, chemicals as weapons, and themselves as combat heroes. When biologist Rachel Carson exploded the myth of agricultural security through chemical aggression on nature, the chemical industry, many scientists, and some politicians saw a woman who had stepped into a world where she had no place and, they alleged, no competence. Theirs was the world of rationality, technology, public policy, and science. Her rightful and most suitable place was poetic nature writing, to charm and console them at home after a day's combat with nature....

> We have been robbed of the history of female technical initiative, imagination, and invention. We have lost our place in defining and shaping technology....

In most developing countries, women tend woodlots, do subsistence farming, and are responsible for water supply and waste disposal. Yet development aid and technologies exogenously introduced have ignored women's knowledge and failed to engage them in the design and use of new technologies. They often destroy the environmental base which has been used and conserved by women. In the so-called developed world, laboratories, research institutes, and companies are modeled on the patriarchal family.... [Women's] bodies are now being disassembled and reassembled by biomedical technologists, who claim to create and control life better than [women themselves] can (1989:9–11).

We are under the thumb of a technological power that is aggressively *masculine*.

### The "Flick of a Switch" Syndrome

The *debilitating* power of technology owes much to what might be called the "flick of a switch" syndrome. Technological devices give us a commodity or function—light, heat, whirring blades, printing, elevator movement—at the mere press of a button. We are left unaware of the complex workings of the machine, let alone the interconnected systems of energy supply and production that are combining to give us what we want. "Between the use of simple techniques and that of modern equipment lies the reorganisation of a whole society" (Sachs 1989:4). It hits home perhaps when a storm takes out a section of the National Grid, though even then we may not consider the way in which the *type* of energy source is determining our lifestyle: nuclear power stations, for instance, require large-scale investment, authoritarian structures, and tight security; fossil fuels lock us into the global policies of multinational corporations, the emission of greenhouse gases, the movement of huge tankers on the high seas, and the environmental and human costs associated with mining; renewable sources, such as solar or wind power, can be small-scale and therefore more amenable to democratic decision making and to linking us with our neighbors. Even if these implications are perceived, the user is left feeling helpless to alter anything: "Our competence has dwindled to the ability to turn on a switch. It is not competence we have gained, but increasing dependence on systems, seemingly beyond our control. With that dependence has come a deep sense of powerlessness and incompetence" (Ledger 1989:4).

The ease of the switch and the hidden machinery also undermines the incentive to share skills and enthusiasms. The user is cut off from the skills of those who have designed and produced the device and from the possibility of sharing their expertise and ways of seeing things. Nor is there much encouragement to go out and find partners to create something of your own: it is much easier to switch on the CD player than to go to a concert with friends, let alone gather a group to make music together. "Technological devices encourage people to become consumers of individual commodities which have lost their connection with the creativity and skill that have made them available and with the social relationships that were previously needed and engendered" (Conway 1992:183, review of Borgmann 1984).

Paradoxically, an instantly available technology can also be experienced as an *exhilarating* power, or "fragile magic," to use Sachs' term:

> Whoever puts his foot down on the accelerator or pulls a lever also commands a remote, an invisible world in order to precipitate an event in the immediate, visible everyday world. All of a sudden, incredible power or speed becomes available, whose actual causes lie hidden far beyond the horizon of direct experience. The firework display happens, so to speak, frontstage, whilst the gigantic machinery that makes it all possible ticks away backstage, out of sight.... The speeding power of the car excites the driver precisely because its prerequisites—pipelines, streets, assembly-lines,

etc.—along with its consequences—noise, air pollution, greenhouse effect, etc.—remain far beyond the view from the windshield. The glamour of the moment is based on a gigantic transfer of its cost: time, effort, and the handling of consequences are shifted onto the systems running in the background of society (1989:7).

Whether experienced as debilitating or exhilarating, technological systems that are available at the flick of a switch obscure the value judgments built into their development. There is therefore no immediate way to modify those judgments. We are left in the grip of seemingly uncontrollable power.

## A Mess of Pottage

The symbiotic relationship between technologies and the dominant capitalist economy has increasingly tied technological creativity, skill, and effort to the production of consumer goods and their vast associated infrastructures. This has perverted the aim of primarily addressing people's needs into that of creating new wants; it has reduced the promise of liberating people to live a dignified life within self-sufficient communities, to that of providing individual choice in a consumer market. Technology has therefore become the engine of a spiraling activity that demands ever more powerful and trendy gizmos, more persuasive advertising, and more competitive marketing. The desires that are targeted are those most likely to keep the spiral going: success, possessions, riches, speed, thrills. The intention is well illustrated by John Staudenmaier when describing the advertising technique adopted by General Motors in the early part of the century. All that has changed is the sophistication of the technologies that are now available for both the goods and the marketing:

> First, they introduced annual model changes. Second, the company began to advertise its products, not as tools for transportation, but as enhancements of sexuality, social status, and individualistic "freedom of choice."...

The simultaneous messages that "new means better" and "the car enhances my inadequate sexual and social status" teach me an essential lesson for consumer behavior.... "I am what I own. But what I currently own is inadequate. Therefore, twitch and buy" (1987:13).

The spiral drags more and more of our common life into itself. We become what Sachs calls a society in which a person-to-thing relationship matters more than a person-to-person relationship (1989:1). In John Cobb's words, we are driven into being individuals-in-markets rather than, much more profound and significant, persons-in-community (1994:10). What this can mean in practice is well caught in a description given by Mark Slouka of his morning journey to work:

From the highway, I can see community after community, each stuffed with identical (and very expensive) houses on a quarter of an acre or less, each with a two-car garage. The postage-stamp lawns are manicured, perfect, and empty. Looking at these communities, one thing is utterly obvious: no life outside the home is possible here. There is no playground, no park, no field or meadow. Children don't play ball in the streets; couples don't scandalize grandmothers by kissing too long and passionately in the shadows of the trees (there are none); neighbors don't talk or even argue. The only option, if you want to go out, is to take a car. So what do people who live in these communities do? What else *can* they do? They live inside: watching television, listening to their home entertainment systems, playing computer games. When they go out, they do so mainly to go in: to a mall, a store, a movie theater (1996:72).

When the ingenuity and skills of technologists are sucked into this spiral, then technology has become a *trivializing* power. We have sold our birthright for a mess of pottage.

## Power in the Making

As technological systems are designed and developed, they
become vehicles of specific forms of power and authority. I
was reminded of this when gazing down at the ranks of indi-
vidually crafted terracotta warriors and their horse-drawn
bronze chariots guarding the tomb of the first Emperor of
China (3rd century B.C.). I was amazed at the technological
skills, overwhelmed by the scale, horrified at the cost in
labor and lives, and appalled at the beliefs that impelled the
design and construction of such an impenetrable defense for
the Emperor's body and soul. I was acutely aware of the
*power relationships* embodied in that enormous enterprise.

I then found myself pondering the structures of power that
are being embedded in *today's* technological achievements,
and how they are determining the control and the participation exercised and experienced in different communities
around the world. Technologies comprise ways of ordering our
lives. They have a multiplying, reinforcing effect: hierarchical
systems, for instance, tend to be chosen by authoritarian management and then breed more of the same. By contrast, wide
consultation can result in adaptive networking systems that
favor and support inclusive participation. This is the origin of
the political dimension of the technological power that grips
us. Langdon Winner has made clear the need to name it:

> The same careful attention one would give to the
> rules, roles, and relationships of politics must also be
> given to such things as the building of highways, the
> creation of television networks, and the tailoring of
> seemingly insignificant features on new machines.
> The issues that divide or unite people in society are
> settled not only in the institutions and practices of
> politics proper, but also, and less obviously, in tangible
> arrangements of steel and concrete, wires and semi-
> conductors, nuts and bolts (1986:29).

In a later passage he describes in more detail the "tangi-
ble arrangements" that have been built up "invention by

invention, industry by industry, engineering project by engineering project, system by system" and the power structures they impose:

> First is the ability of technologies of transportation and communication to facilitate control over events from a single center.... Without anyone having explicitly chosen it, dependency upon highly centralized organizations has gradually become a dominant social form.

> Second is a tendency for new devices and techniques to increase the most efficient or effective size of organized human associations. Over the past century more and more people have found themselves living and working within technology-based institutions that previous generations would have called gigantic....

> Third is the way in which the rational arrangement of sociotechnical systems has tended to produce its own distinctive forms of hierarchical authority.... Thus, far from being a place of democratic freedom, the reality of the workplace tends to be undisguisedly authoritarian.... At the point in history in which forms of hierarchy based on religion and tradition had begun to crumble, the need to build and maintain technical systems offered a way to restore pyramidal social relations. It was a godsend for inequality.

> Fourth is the tendency of large, centralized, hierarchically-arranged sociotechnical organizations to crowd out other varieties of human activity. Hence, industrial techniques eclipsed craftwork; technologies of modern agribusiness made small-scale farming all but impossible; high-speed transportation crowded out slower means of getting about....

> Fifth are the various ways that large sociotechnical organizations exercise power to control the social and political influences that ostensibly control them. Thus, to take one example, psychologically sophisticated

techniques of advertising have become a customary way of altering people's ends to suit the structure of available means, a practice that now affects political campaigns no less than campaigns to sell under-arm deodorant or Coca-Cola (Winner 1986:47–48).

The manipulation of power relationships by the technology employed is not outside human control: the form of the technology is consciously chosen and could be open to debate. The article "Networks for An Open Society" in *Demos* magazine had this to say about decisions facing the government of the United Kingdom in relation to the use of information technology:

> For government there is a crucial choice to be made: whether to shape the government's own data networks for social security, inland revenue, and other services primarily as internal networks for management control, or as media for interaction with the public. So far the choices are being made in the first direction, perhaps not surprisingly given the lack of public debate. Yet there are strong arguments for shaping them very differently—to empower customers and provide a medium for interaction around services such as job placement, health information, tax advice, or complaints (Mulgan 1994:4).

### Keeping Our Distance

One much trumpeted feature of modern information and communication technologies (ICT) is their ability to span geographical distance, making "it easy for players in the global economy to form alliances with other players from all over the world, and to do business with them, without ever having to leave their desks" (Harrison 1995:20). Herein lurks another factor that lands us under the influence of an ambiguous technological power, as Harrison also suggests: "It is the boast of new technology that it is remote technology. So how can we be surprised when it begins to make us remote not just from our desks, but from each other?" (:21).

We can exchange a flood of information but remain aloof from the personal experience and feelings, the genuine hopes and fears, of the other people who are briefly "on-line." This is sometimes deliberate, as revealed in this comment by a company owner during an interview on National Public Radio:

> With the information technologies already available, I can sit on the beach of my Florida home with a laptop computer and a cellular telephone and monitor the video images installed throughout my manufacturing company in Ohio to ensure that my people are on the job and doing their work properly (quoted in Korten 1996:4).

It is sometimes an instinctive defense mechanism:

> Electronic communications media sometimes bring the ghastly poverty of workers in distant lands into our own living rooms. The more we learn about it, the less we want to hear about it.... As it hits the borders of our imagination the flood of information evokes our instinctively defensive reactions (Müller-Fahrenholz 1995:61).

Either way, it can be a *distancing* power that undermines real understanding, solidarity, and commitment one to another. Preoccupation with disembodied instantaneous messages prevents a fully sympathetic response to actual pressing human needs. A prominent Dutch media personality, Albert van den Heuvel, gave this warning to his colleagues in the World Association for Christian Communication:

> In the new Communications World we are content to E-mail letters to unknown persons while a few hundred thousand babies die each day because of malnutrition. That absurd situation should be the first challenge to Christian communicators. Who in our world uses his communication toys for fun only should hope indeed that the Last Judgment is only a metaphor! (1997).

It is this distancing power that contributes a lethal element to globalization: it makes possible the gathering of data,
the transfer of capital, the control of markets, the bureau-
cratic communications within global institutions, and the
management of structural adjustment programs, all without
any "feel" for the highly varied, unique local situations
affected. "A transcendent technology" is one factor ensuring
that "things are no longer soul-size, with multiple voices
attuned to the complexity of things on the ground in places
very different from one another" (Rasmussen 1996:329).
Rasmussen pulls this together with other factors to present
an overall, frightening picture:

> A loose ensemble of free-trade agreements, planet-
> spanning information technologies, and the integra-
> tion of financial markets erases borders and invades
> communities while uniting the world into a single bru-
> tal, lucrative marketplace where all is game and booty.
> Here, in these global management schemes, the
> chains of responsibility and accountability are too
> long and too distant (:329).

### Life's Rhythms

As well as radically altering our perception of distance, technology adjusts our experience of time. "For example," writes
Clifford Cobb, "the whole meaning of time for workers was
altered by the invention of the steam-powered machines.
Work schedules were set by the rhythms of the machinery
rather than by the rhythms of natural phenomena such as
weather and life-cycles" (1992:6). Those schedules were
enforced by mechanical clocks originally devised to provide
more or less regularity to the devotional routines of the
monasteries. "But what the monks did not foresee was that
the clock is a means not merely of keeping track of the hours
but also of synchronizing and controlling the actions of men"
(Postman 1993:15). Technology is now in the process of dis-
solving the distinction between night and day: many industries and businesses are staffed twenty-four hours a day, in

perpetual production and communication for the sake of international market-time efficiency.

Nor is the change of rhythm confined to factory schedules and work hours. There is an accelerating pace of change imposed on those living in the affluent West by a relentless insistence on pushing forward with new technologies. This leads to a way of life dominated by uncertainty and, eventually, lack of commitment:

> Silicon Valley in California is probably the epitome, even the caricature, of a high-tech region.... The most obvious characteristic is incessant change. Technology depends on innovative ideas and new processes to sustain itself and to expand.... An engineer told me, "Things are always becoming obsolete. I've put in so much, but the products are gone. I have a sense of futility."

> Employers are only temporary. Companies are constantly starting up, growing, merging, being acquired and fading away.... Another evidence of impermanence is the obsolescence of employees.... The average high-technology professional will have three different jobs in a ten-year period....

> Perhaps the most frightening evidence of constant change is the impermanence of personal relationships. A high divorce rate and the acceptance of alternative life-styles are indicators of change.... Many people find their personal lives fail to find a dependable base (Larsen 1989:61).

The insistence on incessant change gives rise to a technological power promoting *restless insecurity*, both personal and social.

### Signs and Symbols

Technology not only extends our capabilities, but creates symbols that are the foci and carriers of meaning. The Golden Gate Bridge, the Eiffel Tower, the Taj Mahal, Gothic cathedrals are not just functional constructions; they are symbols of achievement, identity, faith. Berlin in 1989 taught us that even a commonplace technology such as a wall can take on deep significance. This was learned again by ecumenical visitors to Ireland in 1995:

> We were shown only a few of the 16 walls that divide Belfast communities. These walls—some of which looked surprisingly "proper"—have been erected by the authorities to restrain acts of violence. At the outset they served this purpose. However, as members of our delegation from countries with histories of walls (i.e., Germany and Cyprus) would affirm from their own experience, walls have a profound influence on the psyches of communities. One not only locks the "enemy" out, one also locks oneself in. Walls are powerful symbols. They not only reflect a siege mentality, but also contribute to cementing it (CEC/CCEE 1995).

The consumer market too is full of these carriers of meaning. Status and prestige are bought with goods bearing a designer label. We surround ourselves at home with artifacts that "say something" to us or that serve as mementos of people and places. The creation of this *symbolic* power is in the hands of the designers, makers (craftspeople or manufacturers), and promoters who discern—or inspire—the form and the medium that chimes with our feelings and dreamings.

## Closing the Options

Any account of the manner in which technology takes hold of our lives—and the life of the planet as a whole—must emphasize the *limiting* power of technology: when options have been weighed and decisions taken to develop a technology in a particular direction, with stated priorities and specific resources, other options are closed off. The seal has been set on the kind of power that the technology will engender. Alternatives are squeezed out. Ian Barbour traces, for instance, how the decisions of the U.S. Navy to develop a pressurized light water nuclear reactor (LWR) in order to power submarines also determined the designs of the first nuclear power stations and those built during the very rapid upscaling in size and numbers between 1965 and 1970. He then comments:

> Until 1965, nuclear technology still had considerable flexibility, but by 1970 large-scale light water reactors had developed a momentum of their own, sustained by heavy financial investment and institutional commitments. The industry was locked in before it could learn from experience.... Long lead times and huge capital investment in large plants with which there had been no previous experience produced an inflexible system, and mistakes were difficult and costly to correct (Barbour 1992:123).

The dangers of this committed direction for nuclear technology were further compounded:

> The U.S. Atomic Energy Commission's mandate to *regulate* nuclear power was compromised by its conflicting mandate to *promote* nuclear power. The AEC was secretive, suppressed information and internal dissent, and virtually excluded participation by citizens or independent experts. As often happens, a "cozy triangle" of a government agency, a legislative committee, and a private industry shared a common interest in promoting a particular technology (:123)

Not only did this route lead to the Three Mile Island accident; it starved investment in technologies for *alternative* energy sources, which would have been less hazardous and not so dependent on large-scale, centralized infrastructures and secretive bureaucracy.

Today, there are many decisions with regard to the development of technologies that are taking us down the route of globalization. Support is thereby being denied those technologies that would be more able to keep local communities sustainable and ensure a life for future generations. It is a fundamental danger of globalization that doors are being closed against those technology innovators and developers who are trying to pursue their activities in response to the particularity of their own regions and localities.

## Who Makes the Decisions?

I have tried to trace some of the processes by which technologies, alongside their evident attractions, almost by stealth establish a power over our lives and subvert the quality of human relationships and the well-being of the whole earth community. The potential characteristics of this power, always dependent on the complex web of particular circumstances, have turned out to be formidable: the five arising from blinkers—insensitive, marginalizing, immoral, destructive, promoting a masculine agenda; the two related to the "flick of a switch" syndrome—debilitating and exhilarating; and also—trivializing, manipulating power relationships, distancing, stimulating restlessness, imposing meaning, and foreclosing options. Yet the analysis has also implied that the power is not predestined: a technological artifact or system exerts a particular influence because certain choices, decisions, and value judgments are made in the course of designing, producing, evaluating, and using it. Its influence—often subtle and unrecognized—depends, for example, on the priorities and criteria chosen, the purposes articulated, the methods of consultation used, the research undertaken, the sympathies brought to bear, the timescales adopted, and the extent to which the values being built in are acknowledged and openly debated.

The question remains as to who makes these decisions and where responsibility rests for the choices made. Many players have made brief appearances during the analysis: designers, engineers, manufacturers, company directors, executives of transnational corporations, investors, trade-union leaders, politicians, community leaders, waste-disposal experts, bureaucrats, lawyers, economists, consumers, media bosses, advertisers, computer programmers, scientists. The web of decision making appears extremely tangled, which heightens the impression of a power that it is impossible consciously to control or shape. This is a misleading conclusion for two paradoxically complementary reasons. First, there are nodes in the web that correspond to all-important decisions taken by elites in government, multinational businesses, commercial enterprises, and professional service sectors—elites who take a pride in their positions of responsibility and who would not deny that their decisions are crucial. Second, the web is so extensive that few people are wholly outside it. Each of us can find some chance to raise an issue, bring an assumption into the open, change a habit, make or do something in a different way.

For the elite, the challenge is to look beyond their own—or their organization's—immediate interests, of profit or of power; to take into consideration the likely impact on a much wider front, not least on those whose quality of life will be touched, intentionally or inadvertently, by their own choice or by someone else's imposition. It will involve stepping outside slick management procedures and well-worn paths in the corridors of power in order to listen and observe from the perspectives of those at the receiving end of their choices. It means taking their eyes off their own glittering prizes and looking to the health and welfare of all.

For those who are not at the nodes there are still chances to exert pressure on the way the web is being woven. Indeed, taking initiative at this level is vital: "Social change will not come to us like an avalanche down the mountain. Social change will come through seeds growing in well-prepared soil—and it is we who prepare the soil. We also seed thoughts and knowledge and concern" (Franklin 1992:121).

Franklin continued, during the last of her Massey Lectures on *The Real World of Technology*, to press the question as to how we do that. She spoke of the necessity "to transcend the barriers that technology puts up against reciprocity and human contact" and then to find ways of speaking to one another about issues of justice:

> It can be done by considering simple and everyday things. Look at the size of North American newspapers. One needs to ask, "Who has given anyone the

right to cut down trees and destroy habitat for the sake of a double-page advertisement for cars?" These are things that in a oaring world cannot be condoned.... Or one can ask, "Who has given the right to publishers to suddenly dish out their newspapers in individual plastic bags that just add to the already unmanageable waste? Who gives the right to owners of large office buildings to leave lights on all night in their empty buildings?" These are not questions of economics; they are questions of justice—and we have to address them as such.... Today the values of technology have so permeated the public mind that all too frequently what is efficient is seen as the right thing to do.... The public discourse I am urging here needs to break away from the technological mindset to focus on justice, fairness, and equality in the global sense. Once technological practices are questioned on a principled basis and, if necessary, rejected on that level, new practical ways of doing what needs to be done will evolve (:121f).

This already provides an important approach to engaging the power of technology. But first we need to look in a little more detail at the dominant mindset and the worldviews that many of the players in the technological enterprise bring to their decisions and value judgments.

# 3

# Worldviews Governing Technology

We all operate within a framework of meaning, a worldview that governs our outlook and choices, a set of commitments that motivate our actions. David Bosch, the South African theologian, put it this way:

> Worldviews are integrative and interpretive frame-works... by which reality is managed and pursued, sets of hinges on which all our everyday thinking and doing turns.... Worldviews are shaped by both inculcated (or assumed) faith convictions *and* by context, social status, emotional health, and the like. They are shaped by both "theory" and "practice," which condition each other, or, in Christian parlance, by both divine revelation and human experience.... [Each worldview] is both a sketch of and a blueprint for reality, a vision *of* life and *for* life.... It is not the terminus of our quest for insight, but our place of departure (Bosch 1995:49).

### The Dominant Technological Culture

Artists and poets are sometimes able to convey these places of departure, visions of life, more vividly than an attempt at analytical description. The following are three examples that shed light on the worldviews that have shaped much of today's technological culture:

1. In many paintings by eighteenth-century artists that depict the pioneer iron bridge near Coalbrookdale in Shropshire, England, rationality is expressed by the geometrical lines of the bridge itself, but aspects of nature that remain unmastered are indicated by emphasis on the wildness of the bridge's natural setting. Contemporary paintings of the Coalbrookdale blast furnaces often showed them as they appeared at night, emphasizing the elemental force of fire mastered by man (Pacey 1992:181).

2. In his play *Prometheus Bound*, Aeschylus wrote that "all human skill and science was Prometheus's gift".... [But] the Chorus is aghast at the gift of fire. Prometheus tells them with pride that "fire has proved for men a teacher in every art, their grand resource." But the Chorus cries: "What? Men, whose life is but a day, possess already the hot radiance of fire?"

   It is significant that, in the opinion of the Chorus, it was the temporal nature of humanity that made it unfit to be trusted with fire.... The Chorus would not have been surprised that a monumental statue of Prometheus was erected by the Soviets in front of the Chernobyl nuclear power plant; only at the hubris that their warning was ignored. The need we now have to keep that crippled and radioactive reactor isolated for up to 100,000 years violates that very principle of which the Promethean Chorus warned (Pursell 1994:29).

3. Gordon Bennett is an Australian Aboriginal "urban" artist. One of his paintings, which is also a disturbing challenge to a Christian interpretive framework, is titled "Perpetual Motion Machine." On the left-hand side of the picture is a row of identical box-houses from which hang the swinging, laughing heads of white businessmen. In the background on the right are partly obscured words and rows of small black crosses. In the foreground on the

right are the "mimi" spirit figures. The artist himself commented in 1988:

> The concept of a perpetual motion machine I saw as a perfect metaphor for the Western capitalist system and its excesses.... It ploughs ever onward convinced in its ethnocentric values which revolve ultimately around *Logos*—the word of God—colonizing the wilderness and "civilizing" the indigenous inhabitants.

> The heads swing together in the rhythm of perpetual motion. The heads bang together in the "healthy" competition of the capitalist system.... The machine inadvertently knocks over the group of "mimi" spirit figures, thus failing to recognize Aboriginal culture....

> Behind all this is written a passage from Genesis: "So God created man in His own image; in the image of God He created him; male and female He created them. God blessed them and said to them, 'be fruitful and increase, fill the earth and subdue it, rule over the fish in the sea, the birds of the heaven, and every living thing that moves upon the earth.'"...

> I saw this passage as the essence of Logos in relation to colonialism and the exploitation of nature. The crosses are the symbol of Christianity, but also relate to the graves of Aboriginal people in the Northern Territory which... are marked only by a simple cross and a number. Each cross has a number and may be seen as a metaphor for the dehumanizing process of this, our Western culture (Crumlin and Knight 1991:143).

This third example describes a worldview based on what, for many Christians, is a travesty of the Genesis account of creation. However, we cannot deny that "Francis Bacon (1571–1626) claimed that through scientific technology nature can be 'dissected' and 'forced out of her natural state and squeezed and molded' so that 'she' 'takes orders from man and works under his authority'" (Rasmussen 1996:87).

Nor can we deny that the Enlightenment construed "science, technology, and culture itself as the dynamics of mastery and control, with nature, society, and psyche itself as the objects" (:86).

However, the Genesis account can carry a very different meaning:

> Jewish and Christian stories of origin [are rooted] in the strong biblical sense of moral responsibility before God who is the power in and of creation and the transcending power who beckons creation's redeeming transformation in the steady direction of compassion and justice. From this God, we receive the gift of life. Before and with this God, we are responsible for it (:256).

The Genesis story of origin here inspires a worldview that accepts the whole of creation as God's gift to be cared for in the light of God's concern for compassion and justice. It is a calling to human beings to carry that responsibility, knowing they are intimately bound to the rest of creation and its purposes; we are part of the tree of life that needs protecting from our own careless hacking away at the wood. It is a vision that commissions us through a sense of awe and wonder, not hubris.

If we have been slow to catch this meaning and to glimpse this vision, it is because technology itself reflects back into our perceptions the dominant worldview that launched it so successfully in the first place. Having set out to control nature and to construct our own future of material well-being, we have allowed the technological means to become the central goal and purpose we are striving for. Worse still, as Lewis Mumford noted in 1944, "between the 13th and the 19th century, one may sum up the changes in the moral climate by saying that the seven deadly sins became the seven cardinal virtues. Avarice and greed ceased to be a sin.... Greed, gluttony, avarice, envy, and luxury were constant incentives to industry" (Mumford 1944, quoted in Franklin 1992:65). We are apparently prepared to harness any human emotions and passions, and to call them good, if they help us to achieve more wealth or a "better performance." This is the fundamental level of the power that technology exercises over us, making it nearly impossible to see through any other spectacles:

> To put the matter crudely: when we represent technology to ourselves through its own common sense we think of ourselves as picking and choosing in a supermarket, rather than within the analogy of the package deal. We have bought a package deal of far more fundamental novelness than simply a set of instruments under our control. It is a destiny which enfolds us in its own conceptions of instrumentality, neutrality, and purposiveness. It is in this sense that it has been truthfully said: technology is the ontology of the age. Western peoples (and perhaps soon all peoples) take themselves as subjects confronting otherness as objects—objects lying as raw material at the disposal of knowing and making subjects (Grant 1986:32).

This underlines the enormity of the task of engaging the power of technology in order to give it a new framework of meaning and usefulness within God's redemptive purposes for the whole of creation. This is how Charles Elliott, economist and theologian, expresses the challenge:

> The first step in dethroning technology, to chasing it back to its proper place in the order of things, is not to belittle it or detract from its intellectual fascination or its power to set men and women free from drudgery, but, rather, to erect around it and over it other values and wisdoms that oblige us to see technology in its correct perspective. The great themes of the meaning of life, the redemptive potential of death and suffering, the astonishing insights of artistic intuition, the recovery of a sense of the cosmic scale of the human tragedy and the human comedy, all that in earlier ages different cultures have understood by wisdom, and all that is supposed to be reflected in and meditated upon

through religious consciousness—these are the powers that reduce an upstart lust for technique to its proper place (1988:179).

## A Biblical Approach

As in the interpretation of the Genesis account of creation given above, Christians turn to the Bible as the key source of wisdom for developing a critique of technology and of the choices that lead to the characteristic thrusts of its power. So in the following chapters, those thrusts will be set alongside insights inspired by the biblical witness. The correspondence will not be exact: the biblical vision does not map directly onto the myriad of day-to-day decisions in the technological world. But it does nourish our imagination and enable us to see that world differently, which is the necessary "place of departure" (Bosch 1995:49) if we are to "seed thoughts and knowledge and concern" (Franklin 1992:121).

Two biblical themes underpin my approach. The first concerns an understanding of creation itself, in its wholeness and integrity. I believe the Bible shows that humankind shares in the "integrity of creation," which is "the value of all creatures in themselves, for one another, and for God, and their interconnectedness in a diverse whole that has a unique value for God" (McDaniel 1990:165). I also believe that God, the Creator and Sustainer, is continuously present in the ongoing evolutionary processes of the creation, though the outcome of those processes is not guaranteed: God respects both the stabilities and the freedoms of the creation that alone make possible relationships of trust and love (see Cole-Turner 1993:99f). But God's redemptive and loving purposes have been decisively shown in Jesus, God uniquely sharing the pain and the ambiguity of our lives and offering us a way to participate in those purposes. Aspects of this way will emerge as we put technological endeavor in relation to the witness given by his followers to the significance of the life, teaching, death, and resurrection of Jesus.

The second concerns the biblical bias toward the poor and oppressed, set out by Karen Lebacqz in her book *Justice in An Unjust World:*

The fact that Jesus was born in poverty, lived and worked with the poor, addressed his gospel to the poor, lashed out against the rich, and was "poor in spirit" (dependent upon his relationship with God)— all these things are evidence of the centrality of the message of liberation to the poor and oppressed. Indeed, because Jesus himself was poor, for the first time in Scripture we begin to see poverty through the eyes of the poor rather than through the eyes of the rich.... The National Conference of Catholic Bishops acknowledges such a principle when it proclaims that the first test of economic structures and systems in the United States must be what they do *to* and *for* the poor, and what they enable the poor to do for themselves. The poor thus become the litmus test for justice (1987:74, 107).

This approach was followed by Kim Yong Bock, co-director of the Third World Leadership Training Center in Korea at a meeting in Manila in 1986 on "New Technology, Work, and the Environment." He is quoted as saying:

The victims of power and technology hold privileged knowledge not understood by the experts, the scientists, the academics. For they hold an epistemological advantage. The victims have a special knowledge and experience of history, real history, of which those who control are completely unaware. The Biblical message must be understood as the account of what God is doing in the world through its victims (Gosling 1986:xii).

Rasmussen recalls an essay entitled "After Ten Years" written by Bonhoeffer as a Christmas gift for fellow conspirators that passed along the lessons learned in ten years of resisting Nazism:

There remains an experience of incomparable value. We have for once learned to see the great events of world history from below, from the perspective of the outcast, the suspects, the maltreated, the powerless,

the oppressed, the reviled—in short, from the perspective of those who suffer (quoted in Rasmussen
1996:302).

Rasmussen goes on to comment:

Here Bonhoeffer's theology of the cross intersects his
experience. "The view from below" and the cross constitute the entry point for radical critique of the reigning arrangements. They constitute the place to
understand the dynamics of modernity that kill. They
are where the violations of community and creation
are most obviously played out. And they are the loci
for knowing God's compassion for the suffering of the
world (:302).

It is therefore by listening to those on the underside of
technological advance that fundamental perspectives will be
shifted and worldviews transformed. It is the experience of
those who shoulder the burdens, not those who reap the profits, that provide the crucial criteria for a technology that
respects the integrity of creation. It is easy for "winners" in a
technology-based development to sweep along on the tide of
their "success," discounting as "externalities" the adverse
interactive effects happening on "the periphery." But
progress is *not* progress if experienced by a few at the expense
of the majority. The starting point for technological advance
must be the stories of those living on its shadow side.

So it is appropriate to pause and take in one more story,
shared by another Aboriginal artist, Lin Onus, through a
fiberglass sculpture "Maralinga." Painted in black, standing
against a deep orange background, a mother gazes in blank
horror and desperation, her child's face buried in her chest,
hair streaming in a wind.

The devastation and injustices of the atomic experiments at Maralinga in South Australia have angered
Lin Onus for almost as long as he can remember.
Despite protests from Aboriginal people that the site
was their traditional country, and so sacred and also

home to them, the experiment went ahead. This sculpture memorializes the moment of the explosion. A woman clutches her child as the atomic wind rushes at them. The cloud is of perspex with red, white, and blue radiation symbols painted on it (Crumlin and Knight 1991:144).

# Part B
# Insights from Biblical Faith

4

# Dreams and Delusions of Development

There was a time when all the world spoke a single language and used the same words. As people journeyed in the east, they came upon a plain in the land of Shinar and settled there. They said to one another, "Come, let us make bricks and bake them hard"; they used bricks for stone and bitumen for mortar. Then they said, "Let us build ourselves a city and a tower with its top in the heavens and make a name for ourselves, or we shall be dispersed over the face of the earth." The LORD came down to see the city and tower which they had built, and he said, "Here they are, one people with a single language, and now they have started to do this; from now on nothing they have a mind to do will be beyond their reach. Come, let us go down there and confuse their language, so that they will not understand what they say to one another." So the LORD dispersed them from there all over the earth, and they left off building the city. That is why it is called Babel (Gen. 11:1–9).

Jesus was then led by the Spirit into the wilderness, to be tempted by the devil.... The devil took him to a very high mountain, and showed him all the kingdoms of the world in their glory. "All these," he said, "I will

give you, if you will only fall down and do me
homage." But Jesus said, "Out of my sight, Satan!
Scripture says, 'You shall do homage to the Lord your
God and worship him alone'" (Matt. 4:1, 8–10).

## Deceptive Dreams

The urge within human beings to get together to build for
themselves a better future has been a central factor in the
transformation of human society. "Throughout modern history, technological developments have been enthusiastically welcomed because of their potential for liberating us from hunger,
disease, and poverty" (Barbour 1992:4). More than that:

> We have created environments in which life may
> flourish, enrich itself, and grow more complex.... In
> order to moderate a seemingly capricious, and at
> times inhospitable, natural world, we build cities to
> increase our comfort, and control our destinies. We
> manufacture instruments which transform raw mate-
> rials into useful machines. We intervene throughout
> the human cycle to restore health (Waters 1990:17).

Human beings are visionaries and dreamers. In our
dreams we perceive the potential that lies within the exi-
gency of our immediate situation and are inspired to change
it. Such dreams reflect the outlook and the commitments
that are in our hearts. They can be powerful motivators.

Up to the mid-nineteenth century, technology was primarily regarded as the instrument for fulfilling the dreams of
"eliminating needless toil, creating wealth, and shaping a
more just and humane society," the *means* to a good end
(Waks 1994:36). But gradually the conception of technological progress became detached from the enlightenment idea
of social and political liberation, technology itself becoming
the criterion of the good. From being the *means*, it became
pursued as the *end*.

> Industrial societies... pursued this love affair with
> technological materialism. The industrial economy

became the organizing matrix of society and the great
machine produced in abundance. The technocratic
value consensus, the belief in power, efficiency, and
rationality, was accepted implicitly by working and
ruling classes; it became a fixed ground upon which all
social value issues were debated (:36f).

A tower of Babel was well under way. But then the social
consensus, according to Waks, was challenged by the atomic
bomb:

The bomb alerted citizens to the dark potential of new
military technologies. And in the 1950s radio-active
fall-out from weapons tests was discovered in milk. In
1962 Rachel Carson published *Silent Spring*, bringing to
public awareness the environmental threat from even
non-military industrial production.... The Vietnam war,
with its napalm, defoliants, and body counts, strength-
ened the image of technology as "anti-life" and "out of
control" (:39).

The recognition of an underside to the great technological achievements pointed to deep ambiguities in the motives
and outcomes of the dreams of progress that had beckoned
so promisingly. There are echoes of that first tower of Babel
in the following analysis:

Behind [the Fordist mass production and Taylorist
work processes] always lay a very human, though
deeply neurotic, urge for complete control, total self-
sufficiency, utter predictability and extreme standard-
ization, all in the name of a utopian desire for security
and abundance.... [But] the offspring of mass production are numerous and varied. Agriculture reduced to
monoculture [while pursuing] goals of replacing natural processes and products with more readily controlled "scientific" substitutes (chemical fertilizers for
manures, genetically redesigned animals) is one
example. Reports persist of hospitals in the U.S.A.
where nurses must clock time like lawyers, avoiding

any contact with patients that is not somehow "bill-able." Experience itself is made into commodities; it is quantified, standardized, and marketed in the form of theme parks, holiday resorts and package tours, and perhaps, one day, "virtual reality."...

We have always constructed our societies out of the material at hand, dreams no less than tools, though the distinction between the two is not precise (Pursell 1994:117).

Our selfish, misconceived ambitions become embedded in our tools, and our dreams have a tendency to turn into nightmares.

### Voices from the Underside: What Is Progress?

The nightmare is experienced first by those who find them-selves on the underside of the technological "progress." In a sensitive commentary on the way of life of the forest hunters of the Canadian sub-Arctic, pointedly entitled *Maps and Dreams*, the anthropologist Hugh Brody has written:

[In the Indian lands of northeast British Columbia] the developers have many dreams: new mines, sudden energy bonanzas, endless oil and gas reserves at deep-er and deeper levels in the ground, possibilities for more and bigger and grander hotels. They dream of restless, expanding, and remunerative activity in a place that, because of its distance from where devel-opers actually live and its history, seems to have no limits.... Sports hunting is upheld far more widely, and with much greater conviction, than is the Indians' right to land that is their home and upon which they depend for their livelihoods.... The Indians' maps are in the way of the white men's dreams (Brody 1981:277).

If we had an ear for the Indian voice, we should at least be prompted to question the master plan, the concept of development into which so much technological skill and

effort are being poured. But, in general, the builders of the
dream city are too preoccupied with their grand design to listen to those from the shadow side who might throw light on
the folly of the whole enterprise. The voices, however, are
not always silenced. Rasmussen quotes David Korten's
account of the intervention made by a representative of the
indigenous peoples of the Mexican province of Chiapas during the closing plenary of the 1994 meeting of the Society for
International Development:

> For the first and only time in the conference, we were
> hearing an authentic voice of the world's poor and
> marginalized, specifically a voice from a group that
> only a few months earlier had declared war on the
> Mexican Government as an expression of its discon-
> tent. Without accusation or rancor, he spoke as a plain
> and simple man of the desire of his people to have the
> opportunity to free themselves from poverty. He spoke
> of foreign aid that had never reached the poor. He
> spoke of the love of his people for the land, the trees,
> and the ocean. He spoke of their desire to share their
> ideas as fellow human beings, to have their existence
> recognized, to be accepted as partners in Mexico's
> development. He spoke of the people's call for a new
> order in which they might find democracy for all.

Rasmussen then comments:

> The goal [of the Chiapas rebellion] was not to seize
> power to govern the country but rather *to reclaim the
> community*. It did not eschew, but used, modern
> means of communication and a strategy of networking
> varied coalitions of dissent.... Rather than trying to
> find its niche in Mexico's efforts to solve its problems
> by strengthening its role in a global economy orga-
> nized around the needs and wants of a consumer soci-
> ety, it sought to order its own world around the
> organic needs of the community. In the words of one
> commentator, Gustavo Esteva, it was not a revolt in

response to a *lack* of development but a response that Chiapas was being "developed to death"... Esteva's conclusion is that the revolt was against conventional development as played out and planned in Mexico: "To challenge the rhetoric of development, however, is not easy. Mexico's economic growth, the promise of prosperity tendered by the IMF and the World Bank, the massive investment in modernity as an integral element of the war against poverty—these have been cast as truths beyond question" (Rasmussen 1996:128f).

José Lutzenberger, an ecologist and former Brazilian minister of the environment, has reflected on similar clashes between those bent on pursuing the dominant model of development, the drive toward a global consumer market using sophisticated technological systems for its realization, and the skills and aspirations of sustainable communities rooted in their own locality. He then dares to press the questioning:

All over the world today, long-established communities that grew organically, that are ecologically sustainable and that give people a feeling of belonging and meaning are being torn apart. Whether they are peasants, artisans, rubber tappers in the Amazon, or indigenous people, they are all being disempowered, demoralized, and uprooted. When the Indian peasants in Chiapas have to give up [their battle against NAFTA], it is cultural genocide. Every one of those Indian cultures in Mexico speaks a different language, has different traditions, different dances, different music. When they leave, their land is taken over by cattle ranchers and their culture is gone, the language is gone. And a language that disappears is like a species that disappears—it will never, never come back. It is the accumulated wisdom of thousands of years of human history, just as a species is the accumulated wisdom of millions of years of natural evolution.

Shouldn't progress mean increased well-being and harmony and a feeling of belonging for a growing number of people in a more sustainable and more beautiful world? If so, then what we witness today has nothing to do with progress. I suggest it's time to redefine what we mean by progress and what we mean by development (1996:22).

The questioning comes out of the experience of those deemed "underdeveloped," but it is also pertinent within the heartlands of Western culture. It has been taken for granted, for example, that progress incorporates dreams of fast and unlimited travel. The result has been vast acres of agricultural land buried under concrete, cities choked beneath a blanket of smog, spoiled sites of natural beauty, floods and droughts in the wake of climate change, and the loss of quiet neighborhoods where people can walk and ride bicycles and children play in safety. But still the dream is promoted as a manifestation of progress, with expanding economies pushing in the same direction. There will be another 500,000 cars on the streets of Beijing in the next ten years, and 1,200 miles of motorway are under construction in Mexico. Despite the increasing concern of a minority, more and more people demand a share in the dream. A combination of powerful lobbies conspire to hide or belittle the dire consequences. Among those with vested interests are oil corporations and powerful transport groups, governments, and individuals committed to research and development programs, users who place high value on convenience and prestige, and those who stand to gain from a global economy that is heavily dependent on rapid transportation.

The signs are there, however, for those who refuse to be duped by this conspiracy, that harnessing technology in a headlong rush toward globalization as the zenith of progress is a false prospectus. It is running full tilt against the purposes of life in creation, in all its variety, and with its potential for people to live together in the richness of community. The story of the builders in the plain of Shinar is sharply relevant: the Lord condemned their arrogant efforts, using a "single language" to "make a name" for themselves through their own technological prowess. The city was doomed to be

left unfinished and the people scattered into mutual incom-
prehension and broken relationships.

## What Is the Meaning of This City?

The story drives home the questions: What then is progress?
What is development for? On precisely what should our
sights be trained? Jesus was tempted by the Devil to answer
in the same way as did the builders of Babel:

> In the story of the temptation of Jesus, in Matthew 3,
> I have often been struck by the way in which the Devil
> promises Jesus all the kingdoms of the world, and
> Jesus orders him off. The Devil does not in fact have
> the power to offer the kingdoms of this world. They
> don't belong to him in the first place. What the Devil
> is offering is a dream—a fantasy of endless power and
> control. "Forget God and reality and truth," says
> Satan to Jesus. "I can give you the illusion of mastery."
> And Jesus, because he is poor and meek—that is
> truthful—says to Satan, "the world is not like that"
> (Williams 1995:6).

Brent Waters illustrates the two alternatives proffered
first by the Devil and then by Jesus, in this way:

> Self-interest may be used as a dominant purpose or
> image. Our creativity may try to ignore the ordering
> and limiting patterns imposed upon us [by the pur-
> poses and functioning of creation] in achieving short
> term benefits. However, the effort caves in on itself.
> Intellectual inquiry becomes a form of utility rather
> than a search for truth. We exchange a capricious
> nature for an unstable life of violence, injustice, and
> pollution. The machines we build to give us greater
> control over our lives begin to control us. As we con-
> quer assorted diseases, others take up the slack to
> remind us of our finitude. An image of self-interest
> strips creation of its purpose to be good for life. It is
> one thing to pursue technological creativity in our

perceived self-interest, and quite another to seek it
with a spirit of gratitude and service to God (1990:17).

St. Paul puts the consequence of choosing the Devil's
alternative even more sharply: "[God's] everlasting power
and deity have been visible to the eye of reason, in the things
he has made.... [But] knowing God, they have refused to
honor him as God, or to render him thanks. Hence all their
thinking has ended in futility" (Rom. 1:20–21).

To those tempted to set their sights on controlling their
own—or others'—destiny in the image of self-interest, Jesus
says, "the world is not like that"—it's about living within the
purposes of a God who has created the world in and for love.
To those tempted to put their faith in technological achievement as the source and goal of progress, Jesus says, "the
world is not like that"—it is to be received humbly as a gift
from the Creator, and to be used to nurture, and be nurtured
by, relationships of trust and caring. In T. S. Eliot's words:

What life have you if you have not life together?
There is no life that is not in community.
And no community not lived in praise of GOD....

When the stranger says: "What is the meaning of this city?
Do you huddle close together because you love each other?"
What will you answer? "We all dwell together
To make money from each other"? or "This is a community"?
(Eliot 1948:Choruses II, III)

## Building Community

When praise of the Creator leads to a renewed commitment
to increasing "well-being and harmony and a feeling of
belonging for a growing number of people," in Lutzenberger's
phrase, then practical implications for technological decision
making immediately follow. Here is Michael Northcott tack-
ling some of them:

What is needed is a more radical approach to political
economy where local communities are empowered

both to resist the human and ecological depredations of globalizing industrialism, and to foster more humanly and ecologically beneficent forms of technology and artifact production.

Herman Daly and John Cobb advocate the practice of bioregionalism as a way of bringing economic and industrial activities back into scale with human communities and ecological balance.... In a bioregional approach jobs are created locally, and goods are mostly traded locally, minimizing the transport and trading of goods across vast distances and in an anonymous market. Bioregionalism involves a new relationship between the factors of production and the local conditions of the environment and of human welfare so that feedback from the degradation of either occurs quickly and locally (1996:300).

This would reverse the processes by which large-scale production technologies and the global economic system have taken apart traditional cultures and wrecked communities living sustainably within their own environment. But it would also transform communities within the Western industrialized nations, creating conditions where people could once again choose to exercise their skills and knowledge and experience to "build up the common life" (Rom. 14:19).

Technologies would have a different emphasis: wherever possible they would use local resources and draw on local skills; they would be energy efficient and designed to keep pollution to a minimum, encouraged by taxes on energy-intensive and polluting industries; goods would be made that were durable, and that could be easily maintained, repaired, reconditioned, and upgraded; waste would be minimized and wherever possible used as raw material for new production. The particularity of the local would be both protected and celebrated in the artifacts made and the methods used.

There is movement in this direction: the mushrooming of Local Exchange Trading Systems (LETS) and local credit unions are supporting entrepreneurship at the local level. Consumers are increasingly exercising a preference for organically produced food, energy-saving devices, and local crafts. There are pioneer developments in industrial ecology such as this example from the Danish town of Kalundborg:

> There, all linked together interdependently, are a power station, an oil refinery, a chemical company, a plasterboard manufacturer, a greenhouse, a fish farm, and local homes. The power station supplies steam to the chemical company and the oil refinery, as well as electricity to everyone. Surplus heat warms nearby homes, greenhouses, and the water at the fish farm. Ash from the power station smoke-stack emissions is used for cement or roads, and calcium sulphate for plasterboard. The refinery's surplus gas production is used to fuel the plasterboard company; and sulphur extracted from the oil is used for the production of sulphuric acid. Sludge from the fish farm and the chemical company is used for farm fertilizer (Davis 1994).

Rasmussen warns, however, that even more radical change is required:

> Kalundborg half stumbled onto the basic requisite for sustainability: understanding creation, or nature, as a genuine community and aligning human configurations to the rest of it.... On one level this first requisite for sustainability is simple. "Comm-unity" is nature's way. All that exists, coexists. Yet the West, in the grip of a deadly combination generated in recent centuries, now globalized, has not understood this at all. Its confidence in humans as a species apart (some humans more than others!); its confidence in docetic, "ungrounded," denatured, gnostic reason; and its confidence in earth-oblivious economic messianism as a transforming power for good— these, armed with multiple technologies, have all ripped open the seams of the earth, left it bleeding, panting for breath, exhausted.

This combination has been so powerful as a globalizing culture, a set of institutions, and a way of doing things that we must pause to ask yet again what kind of alternative knowledge and socialization are required (1996:324).

Part of the answer to that question will come through a reconsideration of the gender bias in technology, taken up in the next section.

# 5

# Nurture and Compassion

When Israel was a youth, I loved him;...
It was I who taught Ephraim to walk,
I who took them in my arms;
but they did not know that I secured them with reins
and led them with bonds of love,
that I lifted them like a little child to my cheek,
that I bent down to feed them....
A change of heart moves me,
tenderness kindles within me.
I am not going to let loose my fury,
I shall not turn and destroy Ephraim,
for I am God, not a mortal;
I am the Holy One in your midst.
I shall not come with threats (Hos. 11:1, 3–4, 8–10).

Jesus was at Bethany, in the house of Simon the leper. As he sat at table, a woman came in carrying a bottle of very costly perfume, pure oil of nard. She broke it open and poured the oil over his head. Some of those present said indignantly to one another, "Why this waste? The perfume might have been sold for more than three hundred denarii and the money given to the poor"; and they began to scold her. But Jesus said, "Leave her alone. Why make trouble for her? It is a

fine thing she has done for me. You have the poor
among you always, and you can help them whenever
you like; but you will not always have me. She has done
what lay in her power; she has anointed my body in
anticipation of my burial. Truly I tell you: wherever the
gospel is proclaimed throughout the world, what she
has done will be told as her memorial" (Mark 14:3–9).

## The Gender Split

I have already quoted from the Nash Lecture by John
Staudenmaier entitled *Advent for Capitalists: Grief, Joy,
and Gender in Contemporary Society*. In it he argues that
the age of capitalism, linked in symbiotic relationship with
technological systems, has been characterized by a series of
radical disjunctions, splitting a number of previously integrated realities into discrete parts. He reminds us that "work-
time was cut away from life's less-precise rhythms to become
'clock time'" (1987:3). He also examines the division of society into a male domain demanding "aggressive strategies for
conquering the earth and succeeding in the marketplace"
and a female domain providing "the compassionate and nurturing side of the human equation":

In capitalism's two centuries we see an extraordinari-
ly pervasive commitment to separating all that has to
do with *rationality* (work, achievement, competition,
tactics, and timing) from all that has to do with *tenderness* (kinship, affectivity, compassion, and contemplation)....

How has this affected us?... When "masculine" qualities
such as planning, logic, and decisiveness are discon-
nected from tenderness, mystery, and contemplation,
what becomes of public life? Accurate judgments about
strategy, for example, lose their depth of insight when
we suppress grief about the often necessary trade-offs
of our tactics. Planning lacks creativity when cut off
from the vulnerabilities of negotiation.... Living as we

do in a world made small by our communication and transport technologies, a world divided between wealthy and scandalously-impoverished peoples, we no longer have the luxury of trying to solve our problems with exclusively individualistic and competitive strategies. Until we begin again to recognize ourselves as citizens of a common humanity, stressing the virtues of intimacy, kinship, and compassion as well as those of rational planning, we will find the renewal of true hope eluding our grasp (:16,17).

The gender split has been particularly acute in technology, as described in the quotation from Patricia Hynes already cited (see Chapter 2). Arnold Pacey produces similar evidence:

In modern Africa, as in ancient Greece, there appear to be three kinds of values involved in the practice of technology—firstly, those stressing virtuosity; secondly, economic values; and thirdly, values reflecting work traditionally done by women....

Nearly all women's work falls within the usual definition of technology. What excludes it from recognition is not only the simplicity of the equipment used, but the fact that it implies a different concept of what technology is about. Construction and the conquest of nature are not glorified, and there is little to notice in the way of technological virtuosity. Instead, technique is applied to the management of natural processes of both growth and decay.... Appreciation of process in this sense partly depends on accepting and working with nature rather than trying to conquer it, and is a neglected concept in conventional technology. Thus Joan Rothschild has every reason to claim that a "feminist perspective" can help create a "soft technology future" where such values as "harmony with nature... and non-exploitation become integral to technological development" (1983:101, 104).

### Technologies with a Different Voice and Structure

Would the technologies with which we are surrounded today, and which so shape our lives, really be that different if women had been more involved in their development? Patricia Hynes certainly thinks so. She cites in evidence the top ten engineering accomplishments of the past twenty-five years as chosen in 1989 by the National Academy of Engineering. These were: moon landing, application satellites, microprocessors, computer-aided design, CAT scan, advanced composite materials, the jumbo jet, lasers, fiber optics, genetic engineering. She contrasts these with a list of her own: photovoltaics, wind turbines, high-speed trains, biodegradation of solid and hazardous waste, alternatives to chlorofluorocarbons (CFCs), biodegradable plastic, widespread use of integrated pest management and organic agriculture, and an effective male birth control device. She then comments:

> The dramatic differences in these two sets of technologies lie not in their technical and intellectual challenge, but rather in their values, purpose, and design relationship. The former prioritize human mastery over nature and devices for faster, more extensive manipulation of information. The latter tend to work in partnership with nature, to be extensions of natural resources, to manifest consciousness of social and environmental impact, to link the human and natural world.

These differences resonate with what women and men scientists reported in in-depth interviews that probed why they were attracted to science, how they see technology and how they problem-solve with technologies. A significant number of women said that what excites them about technology was making it transparent and accessible to others while men more often cited being excited by technical design and function. When asked about technology of the future, women imagined technologies that linked private and public worlds in collaborative and communication-enhancing ways, while men tended to imagine technologies that gave absolute control, extremely high speed and unlimited knowledge, extending their power over the universe (1994:141).

Ursula Franklin suggests that the experience that women have in dealing with the unplannable (like organizing the home around a small child!) could help the development of technologies that incorporate holistic strategies, allowing for situational judgments:

A common denominator of technological planning has always been the wish to adjust parameters to maximize efficiency and effectiveness. Underlying the plans has been a production model, and production is typically planned to maximize gain....

Women in particular have developed schemes that are not a surrender to randomness, but an allotment of time and resources based on situational judgments.... Such schemes require knowledge, experience, discernment, and an overview of a given situation. These schemes are different in kind from those of prescriptive planning. What makes them so different is that holistic strategies are, more often than not, intended to minimize disaster rather than maximize gain (1992:83).

Franklin then goes on to give a practical example of such an approach, to show that it is indeed possible in today's real world of technology—namely, the inquiry led by Thomas Berger into the building of the Mackenzie Valley pipeline:

The Inquiry itself gathered evidence in many different modes, ranging from listening to native residents in their own community to questioning "experts" on the reliability of forecasts of energy needs or gas reserves. This was a very participatory and interactive process, and it resulted in the recommendation of a ten-year moratorium on pipe-line construction, during which urgently needed measures for the community and the arctic habitat were to be carried out. The report also recommended certain constraints on future technological activities. Thus the Inquiry resulted in a workable plan to proceed with development while minimizing potential harm (:84).

In a paper titled *Will Women Change Technology or Will Technology Change Women?* Franklin wrote: "I am not speaking about [rejecting] technology, rather I am speaking about potentially *different* technologies. Just as those who reject unhealthy food are not in favour of starvation but are looking for a new diet, I am looking for technologies with a different voice and structure" (1985:18).

Nowhere is this more needed than in the development and use of the Internet. Women instinctively feel that cyberspace could serve their "networking" communication style and could encourage creative sharing of experience. But the "voice and structure" is against them. Male interests have driven systems analysis and design and have strongly influenced the use of language on the Internet. Young men are both the proponents and the target for advertising and marketing. Games for children are typically of the "shoot 'em up" variety, and games for adults depend heavily on violence and sex. This spills over into easily available pornographic material and the nastier aspects of Internet-based behavior, such as unsolicited abusive messages that infringe on personal privacy and make women feel very vulnerable. In addition, research shows that women have less access to the Internet than do men, either for leisure or for employment. There is also built-in resistance to the research that might document the bias:

> The opinion of the majority of computer scientists and computer academics is that computing and IT are scientific disciplines and are to be researched as such [that is, based on "scientific" evidence and methodology alone]. Therefore, a multidisciplinary approach to computing research is deemed inappropriate, and the

area of gender and computing, which would not only attempt to explain how computers influence our lives but mainly how women can influence the development of computers and computer systems, is deemed unacceptable (Turner 1998:3).

Despite this weighting against them, women have demonstrated that they can enjoy the Internet and make good use of it. If they participated more fully in its development, a different voice and structure would emerge that in turn would open up new possibilities for women. For instance, information on local health, social, and cultural services could be available to women at home, independent of opening hours and without unnecessary waiting time, and with some interactive possibilities built in. Communication would be user-friendly for women wanting to be in touch with others having similar questions and experience. Women could be encouraged into home-based flextime working, with technical support in place and conversation opportunities to counteract isolation. There would be increased provision for public access to terminals in places comfortable and convenient for women. The irony is that the potential of the Internet would be revealed even more powerfully if it became shaped and developed in response to those currently marginalized. It is not only women who would benefit!

### The Matriarchal Shift

The story of the building of the tower of Babel calls for a halt in human efforts to build a future of our own making, to our own grand, global design. Instead, we are to turn in praise to "the God who created the world and everything in it" (Acts 17:24). This can be a first step in a transformation of relationships one with another and with the whole creation: it will be a converting experience, turning hubris into humility, pride into repentance, individualism into companionship, and self-interest into concern for community.

The prophet Hosea gives us a deeper understanding of the nature of these relationships desired and offered by God. He reveals a God of compassion and tenderness who relates to us as a mother nurturing and caring for her son, who acts with forgiveness, not judgment. It is just such an outpouring of love that is affirmed by Jesus when he accepts the gesture of the woman pouring precious oil over his head, a gesture of more fundamental significance than rational arguments over monetary value and cost benefit. The transformation in our relationships is going to require a profound reorientation:

> The Tower of Babel, that powerful image of patriarchal domestication and dominion, must give way to "greenhouses," that is, to matriarchal images of habitation and nurturing.... Building cultures of habitation and nurturing presupposes what we might call a matriarchal shift in human consciousness. This means not only that women need to play a greater part in elaborating new models and programs at every level of society [including within technology], but also that men must be prepared to change their accustomed roles and behavioral patterns to allow their own female and maternal elements to surface more clearly. Caring, sharing, and nurturing are motherly qualities, but not biologically reserved to women.... The "matriarchal shift" should not be construed as a new war between the sexes but as an option that transforms both male and female stereotypes (Müller-Fahrenholz 1995:147, 154).

It is this matriarchal shift that is essential if technologies are to be developed with a "voice and a structure" that reflect the purposes of a compassionate, tender, and loving God.

# 6

# Letting Go of Control: Freedom for the Other

There was a rich man whose land yielded a good harvest. He debated with himself: "What am I to do? I have not the space to store my produce. This is what I will do," said he: "I will pull down my barns and build them bigger. I will collect in them all my grain and other goods, and I will say to myself, 'You have plenty of good things laid by,... take life easy, eat, drink, and enjoy yourself.'" But God said to him, "You fool, this very night you must surrender your life; and the money you have made, who will get it now?" (Luke 12:16–20).

Seeing the crowds, Jesus went up on the mountain, and when he sat down his disciples came to him. And he opened his mouth and taught them, saying:

"Blessed are the poor in spirit, for theirs is the kingdom of heaven....

"Blessed are the meek for they shall inherit the earth" (Matt. 5:1–3, 5, RSV).

### Control or Release of Hope

Rowan Williams gives a commentary on these two Beatitudes that highlights the sharp clash between a shared life submitted

to the purposes of God and a life constructed in the pursuit
of power and control:

> "Poor in spirit" is a characterisation of people whose
> response to and engagement with the world is not a
> constant struggle for *control*.... We have lived for quite
> a while in a culture which has elevated *rivalry* and
> competition to the level of the supreme social value.
> To be told that blessedness resides in letting go of the
> struggle for control can be profoundly liberating in
> this context.... When we have let go, the Kingdom of
> Heaven is ours—because the Kingdom of Heaven is
> simply the situation in which God shapes and orders
> the world....
>
> The poor have the Kingdom, and the meek inherit the
> earth. What that suggests is that reality, truth, the sub-
> stance of the earth, of our shared life, can become a
> gift as soon as we begin to let go of that obsession with
> rivalry that meshes so closely with a longing for con-
> trol (1995:5, 6).

The suggestion that the meek inherit the earth does
indeed run counter to the basic presuppositions and expectations that are shaping a great many technologies (whether
related to weapons, communications, data processing, industrial or commercial production) that have their origin precisely in fantasies of control. They are developed within a
market framework that assumes that selfish competition is
fundamental. This was revealed in a telling comment at the
end of the last century by the American congressman who
gave his name to the Dawes (Allotment) Act of 1887, which
divided up the tribal lands: "[The Indians] have got as far as
they can go, because they own their land in common....
There is no enterprise to make your home any better than
your neighbor's. There is no selfishness, which is at the bottom of civilization" (Mander 1991:276).

The ways of God are quite different. The Bible witnesses
to a God who has not set up a watertight, inflexible system of

control, keeping a tight rein on the dynamic and evolving creation. To the contrary, there is an inherent freedom within the created order that allows conscious, intentional, and purposive activity and the growth of relationships marked by trust, love, and commitment. In the Kingdom of Heaven, power is given *to* participants, not exercised *over* them. It is to be experienced as a gift within shared life, not to be gained by competition.

If these purposes and ways of God were to shape technological agendas, there would be a radical change in the global culture and in the life bequeathed to future generations. The driving force of economic and technological activity would no longer be "How can I win out over others?" but "How do we ensure a life of sufficiency, dignity, and hope for others?" The present foundations would be shaken and a new hope discovered.

### Rocking Arrogant Self-Confidence

Embedded in the urge to control is an assumption that human beings can stand over and against nature—and other human beings—and "objectively" manage, plan, and order all things, greatly aided by the development of sophisticated technological systems. But this fails to recognize the interconnectedness of all things—that humanity is interfering with a nature that is continually changing and evolving, of which we have only partial knowledge and of which we are an integral part. Everything designed and constructed, every attitude and bias imprinted in a technology, shifts the unfolding circumstances, but not always in the manner intended and expected by those responsible. Global warming dramatically alerts us to this. The limited understandings and sensitivities, the narrow vision and selfish intent, that are characteristic of human beings (in theological jargon, "original sin") are inevitably woven in; there are no perfect solutions within human control.

The "poor in spirit," aware of the delicately balanced interrelationships within nature and the potential for human sin and misjudgment, seek to attune themselves to what can be known of God's more inclusive purposes for the whole of creation. They accept their share of responsibility for building a future that reflects those purposes, knowing that vigilance and reassessment, adaptation and recommitment, will always be needed.

### Day-Care Technologies

A particular example of the consequences of a selfish, "control" approach is the willful blindness in global economics to human dependence on the closed, finite ecosystem of Planet Earth. As long as the optic is that of an affluent elite intent on building bigger barns, the question of the optimal scale of economic and technological activity relative to the total ecosystem will go on being ignored. There is consequently no hope of addressing the urgent issue of genuine sustainability of life for the whole earth community. Herman Daly has this to say:

> Since we cannot go back to the cowboy economy [with a linear throughput as if there is both an infinite source and sink], we have acquired a tendency to want to jump all the way to the spaceman economy [living off tight material cycles and immediate feedbacks, with the whole spaceship earth under total human control].... But, as the environmentalist David Orr points out, God, Gaia, or Evolution was doing a nice job of managing the earth until the scale of the human population, economy, and technology got out of control. Planetary management implies that it is the planet that is at fault, not human numbers, greed, arrogance, ignorance, stupidity, and evil. We need to manage ourselves more than the planet, and our self-management should be, in Orr's words, "more akin to child-proofing a day-care center than to piloting spaceship earth." The way to child-proof a room is to build the optimal scale playpen within which the child is both free and protected from the excesses of its own freedom. It can enjoy the light and the warmth provided by electrical circuits beyond its ken, without

running the risk of shorting out those circuits, or itself, by experimenting with the "planetary management technique" of teething on a lamp cord (1993:45).

Rasmussen spells out the analogy:

> We don't, can't, and shouldn't control all the actions of the child; nor do we, can we, or should we the actions of all ecosystems and one another. The human percentage of NPP [Net Primary Production: the amount of solar energy captured in photosynthesis by primary products, less the energy used in their own growth and reproduction. It is the basic food resource for everything on earth not capable of photosynthesis] is kept low enough for the independent life of those very systems our own lives depend on. Which is to say, we remove grave dangers and give wide margin for errors and accidents that will not, *because* there is wide margin, be fatal for most of the kids, their caretakers, and their environment. Theologically stated: day care gives sin and error room; spaceship doesn't. And the habits of sin and error are quite deleterious enough without being pushed to do even "better"! (1996: 171).

The freedom to develop life-enhancing technologies needs to be exercised in humility, within the "optimal scale" imposed by potentially irreversible strains on the planet's resources and ecosystems. Beyond that, adopting a "wide margin for errors" means rejecting a "technical fix" approach that assumes that technological ingenuity will solve all unforeseen problems and will prove able to keep everything under control. That expectation is too insensitive to the full range of human experience and makes too little allowance for human fallibility.

Examples of day-care technologies include, therefore:

- Technologies that rely on the skills and resources of local communities where feedback and adjustment are immediate;

- Technologies that give freedom to people to exercise their creative skills in the interests of the community of which they are a part rather than in meeting the demands of a faceless competitive market;

- Technology that is designed by those who use it and are affected by it, not controlled and managed by those at the distant center of a gigantic global corporation;

- Technologies that celebrate cultural diversities and are not forced into the straitjacket of a common consumer culture. These are particularly important as they mirror the biodiversity that is nature's wide margin, allowing adaptation and recovery from traumatically changed circumstances.

These are what Ursula Franklin would call "redemptive technologies." She has more suggestions to offer:

Existing technologies need to be reviewed in terms of their scale and the appropriateness of their applications. Initially useful prescriptive technologies are often applied to inappropriate tasks, such as when production models and techniques are used in education. Or the scale of a given technology may be the root of its problems, as one finds frequently in agriculture.... New means of technological linkage need to be explored, which would facilitate co-operation without centralization or oppression by scale.

Some redemptive technologies can use existing technical knowledge in a changed structure and for a changed task. [As a Canadian, speaking in 1990] I hope that the technical expertise of the Canadian nuclear industry will be redeemed by the industry providing teams of experts to safely dismantle nuclear reactors around the world when nuclear power becomes globally unacceptable.

In a similar vein, redemptive technologies are needed to prevent pollution. This will mean redesigning industrial processes, reducing waste, and modifying needs and demands (1992:127f).

An example from the field of information technology is given in the issue of *Demos* from which I have already quoted:

The application of management principles from manufacturing often... shrinks front-line staff and builds up administrators and managers.... Little attention has been paid to other applications of technology which could not only bear down on costs and microinefficiencies, but also improve the quality of service experienced by the clients, by giving more power and discretion to front-line workers, and by freeing resources to help populate the front lines—bringing down teacher-pupil ratios, bringing in more care workers, and employing more people to oversee public spaces (Mulgan 1994:4).

In addition to technologies that release people from overbearing control, there must also be action to put in place the outer limits, forestalling irreversible dangers that technological activity is liable to bring in its wake, such as pollution of the earth's atmosphere, damage to marine ecosystems, and desertification. These dangers require global action and transnational cooperation: "Oceans, genetic diversity, climate, the ozone layer, and even forests and other great concentrations of green plant matter form a kind of global commons that must be treated as such. Global community requires some institutions and policies with genuinely global reach" (Rasmussen 1996:337).

Technologies can then be developed to support the global "boundary" policies, such as this initiative in Japan:

Japan's Ministry of International Trade and Industry established the Institute of Innovative Technology with the explicit purpose of "undo[ing] the damage done to the earth over the past two centuries, since the industrial revolution." The institute is exploring alternatives to chlorofluorocarbons (CFCs) and trying to develop biodegradable plastics, hydrogen-producing bacteria, carbon-dioxide scrubbers, and genetically engineered algae for higher efficiency photosynthesis (:341).

It is, however, important to stress yet again that overconfidence in the ability to control a technological system can lead to dangerously insufficient safeguards against "habits of sin and error." In the light of the nuclear reactor accidents at Three Mile Island and Chernobyl, Ian Barbour has this to say:

> The biblical understanding of human fallibility would lead one to be cautious about situations in which errors can have disastrous consequences. I suggested earlier that the social dimension of sin is expressed in institutional self-interest. It should be no surprise that organizations put their own goals ahead of the public interest or underestimate risks that could be reduced by expenditure on safety. If we live in a world of stark injustice and growing gaps between rich and poor nations, it seems unrealistic to leave out the effects of social unrest and political instability. Nuclear reactors would be vulnerable in situations of conflict, and they would be tempting targets for blackmail by terrorists. Moreover, their large scale and cost represent a concentration of economic and hence political power that makes it difficult for citizens to participate in decisions about them. In short, catastrophe avoidance should be given heavier weight than traditional risk analysis assigns (1992:125).

This is the very least that is required of a day-care technology. But the Christian perspective touches a deeper level.

### The Power of Forgiveness

The gospel is profoundly conscious of the fundamental, universal fact of human fallibility. In saying that we have all fallen short of the glory of God (Rom. 3:23), Paul was stating a self-critical fact. He was also prefacing the good news that human beings can be liberated into a more genuinely human life by

God's gift of forgiveness, and enabled to "let go of the struggle for control" (see Williams above). For the "poor in spirit," the assurance of forgiveness is offered by a God who in Jesus has lived through the exploitation and suffering unleashed in the world, overcome the human tendency to safeguard competitive benefit *over* others, and empowered a new way of living *for* the good of all. Those who accept this assurance of forgiveness are freed to follow in the same path. Having been forgiven, they themselves are able to forgive; having been released from the anguish of inadequacy and failure, they are ready to accept and encourage others.

What the "meek" offer to technological decision making is the readiness to accept human fallibility, knowing there is a God who goes on forgiving and re-creating. And the God who in Jesus offers that forgiveness inspires a new mandate—to direct technological effort, not toward consolidating success or establishing control, but toward responding with care and sensitivity to the needs of the "other."

### False Security

Nowhere is this more needed than in tempering the decision making around the development, manufacturing, and trading of weapons for military purposes, to which an alarmingly high proportion of all technological effort is devoted. In struggles for control within the human community there is a ready resort to violence, with military technologies providing the means to overpower or deter "the enemy." The more sophisticated and deadly the weapons, the more they encourage reliance on the use of force.

The desire to exercise power and control in this way runs very deep. The writer of Genesis symbolizes it in the story of the Fall, including "a primal moment of human misrecognition: the false and envious perception that God is someone to be rivaled with." The Irish Inter-Church Group on Faith and Politics further interpret Genesis 3:

Fundamental in the Genesis story is how alienation from God brings a deep insecurity into human affairs.

Fear of the neighbour, rather than trust in God, becomes a governing factor in human relations.... In this insecurity we do two things: we create our own "substitute" gods [including technological ones], which belong exclusively to us and seem to offer the security we need. And we use our differences from others to give ourselves identity as individuals or a group.... We are what we are because "others" are not what we are—and therefore not so good as us. At the same time they excite our envy, our fascination, and our fear....

So we live defensive lives, dominated by the "realism" of fear. This realism says that we must always retaliate when offended, that we must always look for revenge, that we must always be ready for war, that we must dominate or be dominated. An endless cycle of conflict is created (Faith and Politics Group 1997:24).

The cycle is devastatingly aggravated by technological prowess:

Modern technology is displayed at its most brilliant perhaps in the appliances of modern warfare. The United States government force-fed the military-industrial complex over the past fifty years with huge infusions of capital to enable continual technological innovation in order to build the most sophisticated weapons that could be devised (Shenk 1995:97).

Neil Postman offers an important reminder that before what he calls "Technopoly" gained ground—that is, the culture that "seeks its authorization in technology, finds its satisfactions in technology, and takes its orders from technology" (1993:71)—there were limits placed on weapons by an acknowledged higher moral authority:

With some exceptions, tools did not prevent people from believing in their traditions, in their God, in their politics, in their methods of education, or in the legitimacy of their social organization. These beliefs, in fact, *directed* the invention of tools and limited the uses to

which they were put. Even in the case of military technology, spiritual ideas and social customs acted as
controlling forces. It is well known, for example, that
the uses of the sword by samurai warriors were metic-
ulously governed by a set of ideals known as Bushido,
or the Way of the Warrior.... This sort of governance of
military technology was not unknown in the Western
world. The use of the lethal crossbow was prohibited,
under threat of anathema, by Pope Innocent II in the
early twelfth century (:23).

Vestiges of adherence to similar moral constraints are
present today in the Geneva Conventions and bans on chemical and biological weapons, but there has been no stopping
the arms race in ever more advanced applications of technological wizardry that in many cases involve weapons of mass
destruction. When political leaders choose to put their faith
primarily in the invincible power of state-of-the-art military
equipment, there is no incentive to explore alternatives to a
military "solution" or to foresee the consequences of using
violence to handle conflicting claims and aspirations. But
human communities cannot be healed by technologies that
have devastation and human suffering built into their design
brief. Archbishop John Habgood, former Archbishop of York,
has suggested that Christians have a particular witness to
make in this respect:

> In losing sight of the ultimate aim of military opera-
> tions in trying to create a peaceful, just, and sustain-
> able world society, those who are placing their
> reliance on technological superiority may unwillingly
> betray the end by concentrating on the means. War is
> fundamentally a human problem, not a technological
> one, and a major part of Christian witness in the face
> of war must be to concentrate attention on the human
> factors which cause it (1980:90).

Even the attention to the human factors can be colored
by an overriding aim to use technology in order to gain, or
keep, the upper hand. John Deutch, director of the CIA, in a

speech in 1996 to the World Affairs Council in Los Angeles, "The Environment on the Intelligence Agenda," reported on some of the information gained from spy satellites. He said, "Environmental degradation, encroaching deserts, erosion, and over-farming destroy vast tracks of arable land." Moreover, they "force people from their homes and create tensions between ethnic and political groups as competition for scarce resources increases" (see Richard Norton-Taylor 1996). But it was clear that this information is not being gathered in order to tackle the root causes of environmental catastrophes or to ensure compliance with environmental treaties and international arms control agreements, let alone to protect those most at risk, but rather to protect resources that are crucial to the U.S. military-industrial complex and to seek out prospective markets for U.S. firms, not least for arms sales.

If a group of Sahel farmers living on the edges of the encroaching desert had been listening to Deutch, they would surely have felt a double betrayal: no proposal to modify the technologies that have caused such drastic climate change and desertification, but rather an oppressive confidence in sophisticated technology by which the United States can maintain control over and make money out of the farmers' desperate search for the land and water by which to live.

### Serving the Other

A vicious cycle of conflict can be broken only by a readiness to abandon the false security that is bolstered by superior technological capability. The tide of aggressive militarism has to be turned by a leadership open to the "other," ready to recognize that neither freedom nor security is won for either side by seeking to dominate by brute force. Technology could be given a positive role by channeling resources into those technologies that encourage communication and cooperation, that rely on local skills and insights, that protect the natural environment, that promote health care and education. South Africa, for example, is striving against the odds to do just this—to move from a culture of violence to one of reconciliation and reconstruction. Realistically, this must include a whole set of new priorities for the investment in technology. In the United Kingdom there have been repeated calls by campaign groups not only for a reduction in the defense budget and tighter regulation of the arms trade, but also for a comprehensive diversification strategy, investing in socially useful products that would reduce economic dependence on the arms industry.

The Old Testament injunction that the vulnerable "other"—including the alien and stranger—shall be protected, and St. Paul's "Look to each other's interests and not merely to your own" (Phili. 2:4), need to be taken to heart and allowed to pervade the relationships within which and for which technologies are developed.

# 7

# Just Relationships

"Do not ask anxiously, 'What are we to eat? What are we to drink? What shall we wear?'... Set your mind on God's kingdom and his justice before everything else, and all the rest will come to you as well" (Matt. 6:31, 33).

There was a man there named Zacchaeus; he was superintendent of taxes and very rich.... When Jesus came to the place, he looked up and said, "Zacchaeus, be quick... for I must stay at your house today." He climbed down as quickly as he could and welcomed him gladly.... Zacchaeus stood there and said to the Lord, "Here and now, sir, I give half my possessions to charity; and if I have defrauded anyone, I will repay him four times over." Jesus said to him, "Today salvation has come to this house" (Luke 19:2, 5, 8–9).

All the believers agreed to hold everything in common: they began to sell their property and possessions and distribute to everyone according to his need.... They shared their meals with unaffected joy, as they praised God (Acts 2:44–47).

## Biblical Justice

Justice, in the Jewish and Christian traditions, is the restoration of right relationships, with God, each other, and the

71

whole of God's creation. In the Gospels, "God's kingdom and his justice" is described in parables that explore the dynamics of those right relationships ("there was once a man who had two sons..."; "a landowner went out early one morning to hire laborers..."; "a king decided to settle accounts with the men who served him..."). The emerging picture turns our thinking inside out: right relationships are nurtured by generosity and by a readiness to forgive, rather than by the exact balancing of claim and counterclaim. Justice liberates those who are oppressed (and demands repentance and reparation on the part of the oppressors) not in order to satisfy individual rights, but in order to heal broken relationships and rebuild community. The outcome is to be *shalom*, the Hebrew word describing a community that is marked by "justice, dignity, independence and freedom, harmony and reciprocity, the contentment with 'enough' that all may have 'enough,'" and by relationships of "sharing, mutuality and love" (Jim Punton, quoted in Dowley 1984:7d).

"Modern theories of justice present it as something human beings make and impose for human convenience" (Grant 1986:60), based on the assumption that one human being's right to do what he or she wants has to come to terms with the right of others to do what they want. By contrast, the biblical understanding of justice embraces a more traditional perception that "what is given in our knowledge of the whole is a knowledge of good which we do not measure and define, but by which we (ourselves) are measured and defined" (:58). Justice is experienced primarily as a gift, received from God, that draws humanity into the responsibility of sharing in God's redemptive purposes for all people and all creation. It is like entering into a covenant in which all members of a community free each other for participation in a wider whole, to use the kind of language that Archbishop Tutu has always used about relationships between black and white in South Africa. It is this experience of love freely received and given that challenges technological activity that is conducted without concern for "a knowledge of the whole" and without reference to a transcendent good that calls into question any technology that becomes the all-important goal in itself.

## The Breakup of the Whole

It is therefore of profound concern that the usual procedure of technological problem solving commonly fails to take an interest in the relationships that make up the intradependent whole from which the technology is resourced and in which it will be put to use. Rather, the procedure focuses narrowly on a particular need or market opportunity, ignoring wider issues not mentioned in the design brief. This enables the client, the designer, the manufacturer, or the consumer to deal with no more than a manageable number of factors and to apply a limited range of criteria. When these technologies are reinserted into the full human and environmental context, their contribution and impact are hidebound by their own narrowly defined goals. Partial solutions, however exciting and sophisticated on their own terms, are liable to inflict serious damage on those relationships that are crucial to the health and well-being of all. Clifford Cobb sees this happening in both agricultural biotechnology and in medicine:

> The analytical mode of development has almost completely obliterated the traditional, ecological perspective of farmers who raised a balanced and sustainable mixture of crops and farm animals. The analytical model breaks down farming into a number of discrete practices, each of which is studied in isolation. Inputs are varied according to experimental evidence, often derived under carefully controlled conditions that ignore the range of events that occur in fields. The result is increased vulnerability to drought and pests. Each problem is solved without relation to others, and the solution to one problem may instigate others....

> Increasingly the definition of health in modern medicine is conceived in terms of a series of numbers derived from sophisticated machines. The sense of

health as a condition of the whole body in balance has
been largely lost in allopathic medicine. Modern medicine thus ignores the ability of the body to heal itself
and the importance of social networks in promoting
health (1992:8).

Jerry Mander describes similar damage as a result of
American and Canadian government "aid" given to the
Indian and Inuit peoples of the Arctic regions in the form of
computer training toward the use of computer models for
resource management:

That this mode of wildlife and resource management
has a regrettable negative effect on the traditional
relationships between native peoples and animals is
rarely considered.

Once an intimate knowledge based on close observa-
tion and centuries-old teachings, the relationship
among humans and animals is now based on computer print-outs, and has thus become a fast-paced, objec-
tive, abstract, quantitative kind of knowledge. This is
destructive of Indian cultures and traditions.... But
beyond the damage done to cultures, recent evidence
suggests that the objective-scientific-quantitative
computer management systems rarely improve upon
the native conservation and management systems. In
fact, the modern systems often prove disastrous
(1991:257).

Neil Postman is also concerned at the way the
"Technopoly" culture weakens affirmation of the intuitive
and subjective aspects of human personality and experience
that help constitute "the whole":

Modern industrial techniques are made possible by
the idea that a machine is made up of isolatable and
interchangeable parts. But in organizing factories so
that workers are also conceived of as isolatable and
interchangeable parts, industry has engendered deep

alienation and bitterness.... Technopoly depends on our believing that we are at our best when acting like machines, and that in significant ways machines may be trusted to act as our surrogates.... We have devalued the singular human capacity to see things whole in all their psychic, emotional, and moral dimensions, and we have replaced this with faith in the powers of technical calculation (1993:117f).

## Awareness of the Whole

By contrast, Cobb describes the productiveness of an approach that starts with sensitivity to the integrity of the "whole":

The knowledge embodied in the myths and cultural practices of low-technology cultures is not fragmented and specialized. It is synthesized by individuals and by the groups as a whole. Their complex awareness of the landscape that surrounds them makes possible intricate adaptive responses to change in food supply, water availability, disease infestation, and other crises. Given the increasing difficulty that city-dwelling people are having in coping with similar environmental breakdowns, the adaptiveness of so-called primitive societies should lead us to question the superiority of fragmented rationalized modes of thought (:9).

The tendency to lose awareness of the "whole" reality is seen sharply in decisions over reproductive technologies (such as in vitro fertilization, donor insemination, surrogacy, embryo transfer and freezing, laparoscopy, use of eggs from fetuses, genetic screening). Many of these technologies, in symbiotic relationship with an individualistic culture, apply the "interchangeable parts" approach to the human body, making the parts subject to quality control, consumer demand, and bargaining over rights. But this misses the crucial criterion central to biblical justice—the potential for trust and love within the relationships involved, as John Habgood has suggested:

From a Christian perspective the procreation of children is literally a participation in the creative activity of God. But it is not creation by any means and at any price. Its basis is love. Its means is a sharing by two people of their whole selves. And its result is an intimate relationship between parents and their children, which is a given fact, and in which biology and shared experience both play their part. One does not have to be a Christian believer to see that such a concept of the family has a strength and solidity about it which provides a secure basis for personal identity.... There are dangers in introducing elements of consumerism into a set of relationships so intimate and so personal (1994).

Concentrate on what constitutes just and right relationships within the wholeness of God's loving purposes, said Jesus in Matthew's record (above), and appropriate response to human need will be found. In the case of reproductive technologies, this would mean an overriding concern for the quality of relationships affected and enabled, particularly those that give children their sense of identity and belonging. It would mean addressing wider questions, such as the distribution of power and resources within health care. It would mean rejecting any suggestion that women in poor countries might be used as the subjects of research or as a cheap option for surrogacy. It would mean taking a critical look at:

- the priorities and constraints in research programs, especially those involving embryos, and genetic manipulation;

- the part played by commercial and legal investments in research and treatment;

- the counseling given to those applying for treatment and the support networks provided;

- the language that reduces women to "sources" of eggs, wombs, and babies in the context of reproductive exchanges, under the control of medical science, rather than using language that affirms the crucial and essential relationships developed during pregnancy and nurture (see Dyson 1993:16).

## Common Wealth into Private Gain

There is another face of technology practice that perpetuates injustice by working against the integrity of creation—the privatization of that which we all share, constructing divisible benefits out of what is held as common wealth and dividing up the abundance of creation for selfish gain. Examples multiply in today's economic and political climate:

- There are many technologies—for example, wells, dams, irrigation schemes, sewage works—that have been built to tap and purify the earth's water reserves in order to sustain life. These are being increasingly commandeered by some at the expense of others, and at the price of devastating natural ecosystems:

    Just south of the U.S.–Mexico border, the Cucapá, the "people of the river," have fished and farmed in the delta of the Colorado River for some 2,000 years. Today they are a culture at risk of extinction…. The reason for the Cucapá's precarious state lies in the neon lights of Las Vegas, the cotton fields of Arizona, and the swimming pools of Los Angeles. The Colorado River, the Cucapá's lifeblood, has been so heavily dammed and diverted in the western United States that it literally disappears into the desert before it reaches the sea….

    As water supplies increasingly fall short of needs, competition for water is increasing not only between the human economy and the natural environment, but between and within countries (Postel 1996:6, 8).

- Industrial production has resulted in swaths of tropical forest—and the biodiversity and oxygen they supply to the whole planetary ecosystem—being cut down and lost, for short-term commercial gain.

- Large-scale public infrastructures—for example, for all types of transport and energy distribution—are developed and maintained with public money, but the development is above all a response to the needs of private industry, and decisions are taken without public debate. Ursula Franklin gives this example:

> Canadians have never been asked (for instance, through a bill before the House of Commons) whether they are prepared to spend their taxes to develop, manufacture, and market nuclear reactors. Yet without publicly funded research and development, industrial support and promotion, and government loans to purchasers, Canadian nuclear technology would not exist (1992:68).

The injustice is aggravated when publicly funded infrastructures providing benefits for all to share, such as sanitation, drinkable water, safe roads, clean air, rail transport, even law enforcement systems, are divided up so that they can be sold off and run for private profit.

- Astronomical amounts of public money are spent on arms and military equipment. Ostensibly this is for national defense systems, but overproduction is such that there is now a frighteningly flourishing arms trade, highly lucrative for an unscrupulous minority.

- Patents are being granted on genes, food crops, livestock, and human cells to private institutions and transnational corporations. This allows the corporations to increase their own individual profits by staking claim to the biological underpinnings of our common life. It also gives the corporations legal control over the basic technologies and resources of our food supply and health-care systems.

- Mass production technologies were launched and developed with the declared aim of making liberating and useful commodities widely available, increasing the quality of life for all. However, the reality is a competitive consumer market that turns people into individual consumers with little incentive to engage in cooperative effort for the good of the wider community.

The tendency to bend technologies to the goal of seizing private profit from common wealth has to be searched out and questioned during the initial stages of investment decisions and design proposals. It is necessary not only to devise strategies for this, but also to campaign with vigor and persistence against formidable resistance: entrepreneurs usually find it more profitable to regard questions of justice as external to the project brief.

### Taking Account of the Whole

There are other obstacles to adopting a holistic approach to the design, development, and use of technologies in the pursuit of *shalom*. One is the role of experts in a technologically driven society, as Neil Postman has pointed out:

> The role of the expert is to concentrate on one field of knowledge, sift through all that is available, eliminate that which has no bearing on a problem, and use what is left to assist in solving a problem. This process works fairly well in situations where only a technical solution is required and there is no conflict with human purposes—for example, in space rocketry [though, for the sake of justice, questions should remain about equitable distribution of resources—RC] or the construction of a sewer system. It works less well in situations where technical requirements may conflict with human purposes, as in medicine or architecture. And it is disastrous when applied to situations that cannot be solved by technical means and where efficiency is usually irrelevant, such as in education, law, family life, and problems of personal maladjustment (1993:88).

Ten years earlier, Arnold Pacey was calling for a breach in the barriers with which technical "experts" surround themselves in order that the experience, skills, and aspirations of the "experts" and "users" can be brought together in a creative partnership. Justice is then much more likely to be served:

> When technology is really effective, this is usually because attention has been paid to maintenance and use of equipment, to users' or workers' or patients' knowledge and experience, to personal and social values, to government regulation of industry aimed at protecting health, and equally to the responsibilities of individuals for their own health....

> We need an atmosphere in which wide-ranging, interdisciplinary work or political involvement is not regarded as unprofessional; we need education which encourages the proper exploration of situations before there is a rush to problem solving; we need to break down tunnel vision. Given these conditions, we would less often find potentially beneficial technology turning into distorted, damaging fixes (1983:50, 54).

The Consensus Conference pioneered in Denmark is one initiative that involves lay citizens in the decision making around controversial technological developments (POSTnote 56, 1995). A panel of volunteers from the general public are briefed on the technical and policy aspects of an area of technological development by a range of experts. The panel draw up what they regard as the key issues, interrogate the experts in a public setting, and develop a consensus report that is then released to the press. Biotechnology has figured strongly in these conferences: food irradiation, the human genome project, infertility treatment, and integrated agriculture. But they have also included air pollution, educational technology, and information technology in traffic control. The experience of the people whose lives and relationships are affected has been given an opportunity to count. That is a significant step in the direction of justice.

Langdon Winner has explored this need for technological issues to be publicly debated in an article "Citizen Virtues in a Technological Order." He too cites experiments within the Scandinavian social democracies, including the UTOPIA project of the early 1980s:

Workers in the Swedish newspaper industry—typesetters, lithographers, graphic artists, and others—joined with representatives from management and with university computer scientists to design a new system of computerized graphics used in newspaper layout and typesetting. The first phase of the project surveyed existing work practices, techniques, and training in the graphics industries. The group then formed a design workshop....

The pilot scheme, installed at the Stockholm daily newspaper *Aftonbladet*, offered a pattern of hardware, software, and human relationship very different from that which would have been produced by managers and engineers alone. It allowed graphics workers considerable latitude in arranging texts and images, retaining many of their traditional skills, but realizing them in a computerized form. Project members considered but rejected the pre-packaged graphics programs promoted by vendors from the U.S. because they reflected an "anti-democratic and de-skilling approach."... A diverse set of needs, viewpoints, and priorities came together to determine which material and social patterns would be designed, built, and put into operation.

Another achievement of the "Scandinavian approach" has been to eliminate the ritual of expertise. In the UTOPIA project, and others similar to it, a person's initial lack of knowledge of a complex technical domain does not create a barrier to participation.... Conversely, those who came to the process with university degrees and professional qualifications explicitly rejected the idea that they were the designated, authoritative problem-solvers. Instead they offered themselves as persons whose knowledge of computers and systems design could contribute to discussions conducted in democratic ways (1992:62, 63).

Yet another initiative is the movement to persuade industrial firms to conduct a social audit of the impact of their activities on the lives of people affected: suppliers, employees at all stages and all levels of manufacture and marketing, investors, clients, or users. The audit also investigates possible impact on both the natural and the built environment. The social accounts are then published alongside the financial accounts together with a report on the action proposed in response to the findings.

These kinds of initiatives that deliberately take account of the "whole" make it more possible for technology to serve the cause of justice, both in terms of greater equality and cooperation among people and of greater respect and care for nature. It is also in the nature of wholeness that these two aspects of justice are connected. Stated negatively, technologies that embody unequal power relationships tend to be linked with technologies that disrupt natural ecological systems and vice versa (e.g., large-scale lumbering technologies that are employed to cut down large expanses of tropical forest over the protests of indigenous and environmental groups). In the development of redemptive technologies it is important that the link is recognized and tackled.

### Social Justice and Eco-Justice: All Part of the Same Whole

The challenge has been set out by one group meeting at the Assembly of the World Council of Churches in 1991:

> Pursuing justice requires us to learn new ways of paying attention to all creation—the land, water, air, all people, plant life, and other living creatures. A new vision will integrate our interdependent ecological, social, economic, political, and spiritual needs. We want to say as forcefully as we can that social justice

for all people and eco-justice for all creation go together. Social justice cannot happen apart from a healthy environment, and a sustainable and sustaining environment will not come about without greater social justice.... The biblical concept of justice recognizes the need for healthy relationships in creation as a whole. This way of viewing justice helps us to understand the linkage between poverty, powerlessness, social conflict, and environmental degradation (1991:55).

As regards technologies, a variety of responses to the challenge have been briefly mentioned at different points in this book. Here are some of the suggestions that have emerged:

- A move to bioregionalism, with more deliberate use of local skills and resources, and celebration of cultural diversity.

- Investment in companies working on simple, small-scale technological products that can be widely available in the community.

- Locally based information and communication systems, with particular regard to the interests and concerns of women.

- Communication technologies used for two-way listening and sharing of experience (e.g., video conferencing, phone-ins), not just for one-way control in the manner of the company owner on the beach in Florida monitoring his employees in Ohio.

- Information technology used to free "front-line" staff rather than to reinforce centralized control. Flexibility incorporated so that situational judgments can be made (e.g., giving the local bank manager access to information while still allowing him or her to come to his or her own judgments based on personal experience).

- More public participation, particularly of women, in decisions that influence and regulate technological developments. Mechanisms that enable developments to be halted when seen to be serving purely sectional interests and short-term benefits.

- Investment in the technology of photovoltaic cells and other alternative sources of renewable energy. Investment in research on energy storage and on electric-powered vehicles.

- Policies and technologies encouraging energy conservation (e.g., power plants using waste heat from industry, technologies to make homes and offices weather-tight, the development of energy-efficient technologies ranging from more efficient wood stoves to cars that are supereconomical on fuel, the use of microelectronics to enforce road pricing aimed at reducing the volume of traffic).

- Goods designed to enable long-term maintenance, repair, reuse and recycling; also much reduced packaging.

- Technologies and processes that reduce and monitor the release of greenhouse gases and other polluting wastes.

- Technologies that help distribute and save water efficiently and equitably.

- Technologies that address the long-term needs of local communities for food security and health care rather than the needs of multinational food and drug corporations for profitable markets. The priority for sustainable agriculture, for instance, may well prove to be intercropping and crop rotation rather than genetically modified crops, which in any case should be introduced only after extensive research on their potential interaction with other plants and wildlife, and with due regard to the livelihoods, experience, and prime responsibility of local farmers.

- Technologies associated with community activities that provide possibilities of friendship and worthwhile

experience in circumstances where other technologies
are pushing people into isolation and trivial pursuits.

- Arms manufacturers using the skills and imagination of
their staff to convert existing plants into production
lines for the manufacture of socially useful products.

### Participation in Love and Justice

These alternative technologies are developed by those who
refuse to allow the present dominant technologies and their
associated culture to set the agenda. They are developed by
those whose hopes and expectations are formed out of
shared experience with others and sensitivity to the intradependent wholeness of life; by those whose priorities are set
by participating in relationships marked by love and justice;
by those whose making and doing, even their buying and
selling, is a response to the experience of living by grace and
forgiveness.

It is just such a response that is shown us in the story of
Zacchaeus. The outcome of his encounter with Jesus is a
massive redistribution of his accumulated riches to those living in poverty, and an initiative to right the relationships he
had abused. But Zacchaeus' voluntary act of reparation was
not in response to a judge's sentence or to the bottom line of
a balance sheet, but to an experience of friendship that was
both affirming and demanding—an opportunity to learn "the
nature of things through love" (Grant 1986:60):

Justice issues out of that encounter, out of relationship. Biblical justice is not primarily propositional. It
is not expressed in formulas ("give to each according
to..."). At root the biblical idea of justice is fidelity to
the demands of a relationship (Lebacqz 1987:83).

Technologies that contribute to justice are those that are
designed to foster respect, understanding, and trust; that
encourage solidarity and caring; that guard and celebrate
diversity; that enable responsible stewardship rather than
exploitation; that meet needs rather than creating wants;

that are designed with the paramount question in mind: How will this technology help to serve the righting of relationships within the human community and with nature? These are the technologies that nudge us nearer the sharing and unaffected joy that characterized the earliest Christian community (Acts 2:47).

# 8

# Communication that Matters

You say,... "when the raging flood sweeps by, it will not touch us; for we have taken refuge in lies and sheltered behind falsehood." Therefore these are the words of the Lord GOD:... I am laying a stone in Zion,... a precious corner-stone well founded;... I shall use justice as a plumb-line and righteousness as a plummet (Isa. 28:15–17).

In the beginning the Word already was. The Word was in God's presence, and what God was, the Word was. He was with God at the beginning, and through him all things came to be.... So the Word became flesh; he made his home among us, and we saw his glory, such glory as befits the Father's only Son, full of grace and truth (John 1:1–3, 14).

Christian community is about being given the courage to sustain truthful relationships (David Stevens, General Secretary of the Irish Council of Churches).

### Sustaining Truthful Relationships

Communication technologies deal with the lifeblood of meaningful human existence. It is through communication that we sustain relationships, create community, and discover identity. "A person is a person because of other people," so runs the Zulu proverb. Therefore the means by which we communicate one with another crucially affects who we are and who we become. If the incredible explosion of technological "means" of communication is affecting the "end," is there a danger that "the courage to sustain truthful relationships" may be undermined?

One aspect of this question is examined by Staudenmaier in the course of tracing the gradual transition from an interactive relationship between speaker and listener (exemplified in the music hall or theater of the mid-nineteenth century when audiences participated with gusto) to the one-way relationship experienced through the TV:

> By the 1870s the telegraph-based wire services began to provide local papers with national and even international news one day after the event; it was, to put it mildly, an extraordinary broadening of human consciousness as local readers began to be transformed into citizens of the wide world. Still, the transition carried a high price tag. The audience, no longer in any position to interact with the now-distant storyteller or to critique the public version of events, has been rendered totally passive....

> While children learn the passivity required to survive the TV system (i.e., talking back to the TV is fruitless and frustrating behavior), they also learn deep-seated ambivalence about their capacity to create talk that matters. It is no small matter, doubting our capacity for meaningful talk. Lacking such conviction, we tend to ignore our inner life and to treat our creative potential with contempt. All of us learn, too, that the really important news happens on the media and not in our personal lives (1987:11).

Television's one-way communication is not the only ICT (Information and Communication Technology) that leads us to doubt that we might have something significant and creative to contribute. Geoff Mulgan (1994) has insisted that

ICT networks are inescapably interactive, but James Woudhuysen (1994) warns to the contrary. The hope that networks would allow consumers to be consulted, to formulate ideas, and to influence design has failed to materialize:

> All that is held out to us is a world where we can stare at screens all day, communicating, computing, and indulging in "edutainment": not making things, but rather Cruising the Net.... So even in IT there has grown up a complacent culture of diminished ambitions.... It denigrates human beings and their talent to change the real world (:7).

There is another way in which communication technologies weaken our confidence in having something worthwhile to say and to do—the images that can now be flashed all over the world and with which we are continually flooded. These carry intense emotional appeal but usually bear little relation to the world as we experience it, even sometimes to the lives of the people and the events being portrayed. What is transmitted has been selected, edited, and staged into images that create what Ursula Franklin calls "pseudorealities" (1992: chap. 2). In news reporting, "the unusual has preference over the usual. The far away that cannot be assessed through experience has preference over the near that can be experienced directly" (:42). There is the illusion of "being there," though what is seen and heard is only what the reporter and producer have clipped. The spin doctors are able to determine the character of political leaders. "The reconstructed world of images has taken over much of our vernacular reality, like an occupation force of immense power" (:44), and part of that power is in the gulf between the pseudoreality and our own experience:

> What does it mean for us to live in a society whose public voices and stories sound so utterly unlike our own?... The courage, hope, and sense of humour needed to tell our true stories often wither in the presence of the media's implacably well-crafted voice (Staudenmaier 1987:12).

When modern communication technologies cause "ordinary" people to stammer over telling their own story, to lose confidence in their ability to create talk that matters, and to become reluctant to respond with concern and enthusiasm, then the sustaining of truthful relationships is threatened. Equally crucial, the ability to listen is also under threat from one-way communication in which the interactive give-and-take is missing:

> Where there is no reciprocity, there is no need for listening. There is no need to understand or accommodate. For kids this can mean that one doesn't have to be moderately civil to one's younger sister because she is the only one to play with; television allows entertainment without the co-operation of anyone. In school there is no argument or negotiation with the computer.... Women who work in automated offices often report how much human isolation the automated office has brought for them. When work isn't shared, the instruments of co-operation—listening, taking note, adjusting—atrophy like muscles that are no longer in use (Franklin 1992:51).

Faced with such tendencies to isolation, meaninglessness, passivity, and apathy, if members of the Christian community are being given the courage to sustain truthful relationships, they will be learning to affirm, listen, and respond. There are some communication technologies that can help; they are not all one-way and belittling. Ursula Franklin gives this example:

> Even in the universe of constructed images and pseudorealities there still exists a particular enclave of personal directness and immediacy: the world of the ham-radio operator. It is personal, reciprocal, direct, affordable—all that imaging technology is not—and it has become in many cases a very exceptional early warning system of disasters. It is a dependable and resilient source of genuine communication. I am citing

this example so as not to leave the impression that the technological reduction of meaningful human contact and reciprocal response is inherently inevitable (1992:51).

### Opposing the Networks of Lies

It is the other end of the scale, the use of communication technologies for deceptive propaganda, that gives rise to Geiko Müller-Fahrenholz's hard-hitting subhead "Opposing the networks of lies":

> Throughout the third world, television manifests itself as the most subtle of all powers, for it introduces a distorted image of reality into the houses and shacks and thus the hearts and minds of the poor. Critical media education is extremely difficult in the affluent sectors of the societies of the North; in the increasingly impoverished regions of the world, where education is often rudimentary, it seems well-nigh impossible. Soap operas and violent thrillers are essentially deceptive in themselves. But when this escapist programming is combined—in the slums of Bogota or Lagos, or in the tent of a semi-nomadic desert family—with advertising for products whose price makes them unattainable and with government propaganda masquerading as news, an additional dimension of deception and confusion is created (1995:86).

Isaiah's warning is directly relevant: life together cannot be founded on a pack of lies, only on justice and righteousness. It is striking that it is women's groups committed to social change in Latin America that have countered the deception by themselves using media technology (video, audiovisual material, TV) in alternative forms of grassroots education. But their bid for truthful communication has a mountain to climb in confronting the power of mass media technologies shaped by the vast commercial interests of the corporate owners.

### The Wisdom and the Knowledge Lost in Information

Neil Postman graphically describes what is now available at the touch of a switch:

> From millions of sources all over the globe, through every possible channel and medium—light waves, airwaves, ticker tapes, computer banks, telephone wires, television cables, satellites, printing presses—information pours in. Behind it, in every imaginable form of storage—on paper, on video and audio tape, on discs, film, and silicon chips—is an ever increasing volume of information waiting to be retrieved (1993:69).

He then puts his finger on the problem:

> The milieu in which Technopoly flourishes is the one in which the tie between information and human purpose has been severed, i.e., information appears indiscriminately, directed at no one in particular, in enormous volume and at high speeds, and disconnected from theory, meaning, or purpose (:70).

T. S. Eliot summed this up in his much quoted questions:

> Where is the wisdom we have lost in knowledge?
> Where is the knowledge we have lost in information?
> (Eliot 1948:Chorus I)

The response to these questions has two facets. One is to acknowledge that "there are very few political, social, and especially personal problems that arise because of insufficient information" (Postman 1993:60). It therefore is nonsense to equate human progress "with the sheer tonnage of information we are able to receive" (Slouka 1996:125). Nonetheless, once information is seen for what it is, the other facet is to explore how the breathtaking ICT resources can appropriately be brought into the service of sustaining truthful relationships and life in community.

Both facets should be at the heart of any ICT education, whether for children or adults. Through critical reflection, users can be helped to recognize that information is useful only when handled within a framework of understanding forged out of life's wider experiences. The onus is on the users to formulate the questions and shape the purpose, particularly when information processing and rapid communication are being promoted as worthy ends in themselves. Debate can be encouraged, among people more representative than the limited circle of "experts," about where it is all leading and what the criteria for further development of ICT should be, particularly when it is suspected that the design of hardware and software is being geared more to market share and profit margins than to the value of what is enabled.

For ICT to serve the needs of the wider community, increased accessibility and training are required, locally based, along the lines already suggested in response to the needs of women. But it is vital that the training does not just cover technical skills, but builds up the users' confidence in judging where the use of ICT is appropriate. The twist is that the very speed and power of computing systems make the time for reflection virtually nonexistent. Indeed, in many work situations, new and more complicated tasks are demanded, more decisions per minute are required, and supervision is becoming tighter. These are hardly the conditions conducive to thoughtful appraisal of the ideology that is being unwittingly accepted!

One aspect of the ideology that is particularly subtle relates to ICT's fundamental methodology: reality is disassembled and coded into "bits" of information that can then be manipulated by a program, incorporated into a system, transmitted, recoded, or reassembled. These are ideal procedures for instrumental control. Initially, systems were structured along the hierarchical lines characteristic of industrial control and management. But more "ecological" systems are now possible in which bits of information are processed in relational, holistic ways, reflecting the workings of nature. Forms of life can therefore be treated in the same way as nonliving material resources and artifacts, bringing them too under human control:

In the Information Age, the world—all of it—is rendered a series of systemic problems and solutions. The people who count most are those who understand systems and have access to information. The rest is important, but only as "resources." Power is "effective communication," whether the language is biology or engineering or both together (Rasmussen 1996:71).

This way of operating, and the ideological frame of mind that underpins it, is disastrous for the sustaining of just, truthful relationships. Human "experts" end up organizing the ICT systems in holistic and relational ways, but not in order to exercise responsible care for the whole, to free "the other" and build community; their aim is to exploit and manage "resources" (including living beings, organic matter, and the dynamic processes of nature) in the light of their own sectional interests, be they individual or corporate.

For the information revolution to serve the cause of justice and truth, there must be conscious recognition of this bias toward instrumental control. Contributing to the bias is the remoteness of information processing from the reality it is handling. Part of this remoteness is in the nature of ICT: its data are abstracted and coded. But part is in the lifestyle of those who lead the developments and who stand most to gain:

> A new (life-style) stratum [develops], linked by jet, modem, fax, satellite, and fiber-optic cable to the great commercial and recreational nodes of the world, a stratum that no longer need even pass through neighborhoods of urban decay on the way to and from work morning and evening…. In the name of "quality of life," (these fortunate secessionists) can choose their own personal Valhallas and leave the unfortunate to deal with crime, crowded schools, and toxic wastes…. Earth's distress is at a great remove in the same moment that earth-abstracted data are handled in ways that mimic "ecological" patterns of complex interrelatedness.

Through intensification of complex global systems, (the information revolution) appears to push the consequences of decisions still further from sight and thus dims down personal responsibility so as hardly to be felt in the gut at all.... It intensifies the dynamics of a globalizing economy in ways that treat the planet as a commons for the taking, anywhere, anytime (Rasmussen 1996:71,72).

In her Massey Lectures, Ursula Franklin made the suggestion that a job-related constraint should be written into job descriptions, requiring an applicant to use the facilities he or she directs: "Requiring those whose work has a major impact on people's lives to experience some of the impact is really not too much to ask" (1992:125). Could there be similar imaginative suggestions that would help those at the forefront of ICT applications to keep in touch with the people and the situations they are manipulating and controlling, even to experience what it is like to "stand in their shoes"? It is from that experience, rather than from databases and processing chips, that knowledge and wisdom will grow.

### Community in Cyberspace?

ICT itself offers a way to "keep in touch"—the Internet. So what quality of community is offered in cyberspace? Is it likely to help sustain truthful relationships? How does communicating through the Internet shape up to the criterion of *shalom*?

At the level of E-mail, what is offered is a speeding-up of two-way written communication over large geographical distances. How much is communicated and genuinely shared in this way depends relatively little on patterns imposed by the medium; it depends much more on the attitudes and commitments of the correspondents. So for those who have the access and a registered address (and that is still a very small minority of the world's people), E-mail is proving a quick way to keep up relationships and receive news directly. But with dependence on the written word, no face-to-face contact, and very limited access, this falls far short of nurturing *shalom*.

At a much higher level of complexity, cyberspace opens up the possibility of meeting, of acting and reacting, in a "virtual reality" that is continuously evolving out of the product of human imagination and computing skills. It is a world of multiple voices:

> In the anarchy of the Internet, every voice can speak. And on the Internet, those who have ears to hear can hear. Every group—whatever its ideology, whatever its commitments—can stake out a corner. Its message can be made available for anyone who wants to search it out or who just happens to stumble over it. The pluralization proceeds to the point that everyone can have a web page, can tell his or her own story, promote his or her own version of the truth for all the world to hear (Lochhead 1997:102).

Paradoxically, in this pluralistic world in which "everyone" (i.e., the few "haves" with access) is given his or her own space, the break with physical reality is much more marked and can exacerbate a profound feeling of meaninglessness. After all, "human beings and human societies have traditionally found their identities within spatial and temporal limits. They have lived, acted, and found meaning in a particular place at a particular time" (Winner 1986:116). Freed from those limits, there is precious little to hold onto. Responsibility one for another also weakens without this essential rootedness, as Winner finds illustrated in the behavior of transnational corporations:

> In the past corporations have had to demonstrate at least some semblance of commitment to geographically based communities; their public relations often stressed the fact that they were "good neighbors." But in an age in which organizations are located everywhere and nowhere, this commitment easily evaporates. A transnational corporation can play fast and

loose with everyone, including the country that is ostensibly its "home" (1986:117).

Mark Slouka is even more grave in his warning:

It is the physical facts of birth and pain and pleasure and death that force, and indeed enable, us to make value judgments: this is better than that. Nourishment is better than hunger. Compassion is better than torture. Virtual systems, by offering us a reality divorced from the world, from the limits and responsibilities of presence, offer us as well a glimpse into an utterly amoral universe (1996:12).

The danger is that cyberspace becomes the creation of those who feel themselves young adventurers cut loose from the familiar norms and structures of authority and who are seized by the impulse to try anything at the whim of selfish fancy. Like the prodigal son, they claim the right to take the inherited wealth and to spend it in exploring new territory unconstrained by a commonly accepted basis for moral behavior, let alone by a shared understanding of goodness given through "knowledge of the whole" (Grant 1986:58). But it is a claim such as this that comes under condemnation in the story of the Fall: "In the Genesis myth what is condemned is the taking not of power but of knowledge of good and evil into one's own hands, so as to become *as* gods, determining the moral values for oneself and running the show for one's own benefit" (Robinson 1983:6).

Cyberspace run as a pluralistic, anarchical show is not a superhighway leading us toward *shalom*. It is too distant from the fullness of the person-to-person relationships that make us who we are. It is too remote from the joys and the sufferings of life together on an incredibly beautiful but highly damaged earth. It is too oblivious to the responsibilities that life lays upon us. Where do we start, in that case, "making our way back from the virtual brink"? Mark Slouka answers unequivocally. We begin

by recognizing that truth and a respect for truth are
somehow linked to a respect for reality, and that
respect for reality depends on a life lived close to the
physical world. What we need, in other words, is a revolution, in sensibility as well as in life-style,... capable
of reconnecting us to essential things—the things, that
is, we can experience directly for ourselves, not
through the mediating influence of technology
(1996:135).

As in other aspects of ICT, part of the essential equipment
for journeys in cyberspace is the knowledge that grows from
shared experience in the immediate physical world. It is here
that we learn the constraints necessary to nurture relationships of love and mutual freedom. Those equipped with this
knowledge can surf the net, exploring its mines of information and rich varieties of communication, while holding it
within a wider framework of meaning and purpose. This is
the basis of the enjoyment of the Internet described in
Chapter 5 in respect of women. Those who are not so
equipped will only give full rein to anarchy and futility.

Crucially, it is in the "real" immediate world of human
experience that "the wisdom and the knowledge of God"
(Rom. 11:33) has become known to us. It was not in the rar-
efied atmosphere of philosophical discussion, or through
building utopian "castles in the air," but in the social, political, and religious tangles of Palestine two thousand years ago,
among those who came to trust him and those who did not,
that Jesus revealed the redemptive and loving purposes of
God: "The Word that was with God at the beginning...
became flesh and made his home among us" (John 1:2, 14).
To the eyes of faith, it is all that Jesus demonstrated in an
earthly life that is the beginning of knowledge and wisdom:
"The light which is the knowledge of the glory of God in the
face of Jesus Christ has shone upon us" (2 Cor. 4:6).

But this is a wisdom that calls into question the wisdom(s)
that drive many aspects of the information revolution.

Rasmussen finds that powerfully stated in the cross-centered theology of Luther:

> Luther's attention to the cross is a certain way of look-
> ing reality in the eye.... The cross is the symbol that
> shatters humanly generated coherences in reading the
> world.... Faith is the great unknowing, avoiding the
> pretense that lays our truth upon reality in the hopes
> of controlling it.... Luther's confidence is thus not in
> reason's grip on the world as abstracted from its suf-
> fering, but in identifying with the ways of a passionate
> and compassionate God who knows earth's distress
> from the inside out. And this Luther sees in Jesus of
> Nazareth, even in Jesus' death by torture (1996:288).

The wisdom of God is learned *not* by laying *our* truth upon reality in the hopes of controlling it, but in responding to the testimony of those who experienced the life, death, and resurrection of Jesus at firsthand. It is a wisdom "learned in suffering, expressed as empathy and compassion, and deeply sensed and felt" but which in Jesus "wins space for joy and abundant life" (:287). Or, as Hans-Ruedi Weber has expressed it:

> It is not laws and codes that let us discern what is ulti-
> mately good and evil but, as the apostle Paul wrote,
> our conformity with the mind of Christ (Phil. 2:5), our
> following the way of Jesus.... The search for wisdom
> finally narrows down to the question of what is the
> mind and way of Jesus? The answer from the gospels
> is clear: it is the mind of loving self-giving for others;
> it is the way to the cross (1981:101).

Wisdom is learned as we risk following in our own lives the way of the cross, which cannot but take us into the depths of human communication. Insofar as Christians begin in this way to conform to the mind of Christ, they bring wisdom into activities on the Internet, holding their celebration and care for the "physical" communities of which they are a

part together with their appreciation of the relationships that are enabled by the spanning of time and space in cyberspace. It is those who have learned to discern signs of the Spirit in the "reality" of "flesh and blood" relationships who will be able to find on the Internet "traces of Pentecost within the cacophony of Babel" (Lochhead 1997:106).

# 9

# Learning In and For Community

"Everyone who... hears my words and acts on them—...
He is like a man building a house, who dug deep and
laid the foundations on rock. When the river was in
flood, it burst upon that house, but could not shift it,
because it had been soundly built. But he who hears
and does not act is like a man who built his house on
the soil without foundations. As soon as the river burst
upon it, the house collapsed, and fell with a great
crash" (Luke 6:47–49).

## The Aims of Technology Education

At the start of her Massey Lectures, Ursula Franklin spoke of
technology as having "built the house in which we all live"
and of the house "continually being extended and remodeled"
(Franklin 1992:11). What I have been addressing in this book
are the foundations: the fundamental perspectives and commitments that determine the design of the extensions and
adaptations, the life being created within the walls, and ultimately whether the walls continue to stand. If the foundations of future extensions are to be deep enough, the kind of
technology education offered to young people is crucial:

Technology based on the simplistic change-equals-
growth-equals-progress paradigm constituted "a reckless

incursion into the future."... It must be a spur to a different way of using knowledge as wisdom and to seeing our sojourn here as a trusteeship—a cooperative and constructive endeavor rather than a competitive struggle. It goes to the heart of how we see ourselves and, therefore, of how we should educate our children (Tomlinson 1990:16).

Or, as Bryan Chapman has expressed it: "Do we really want to educate young people so that they can deploy their technological skills on the trivia of affluence?... Or do we want to educate them for a world in which, if they do become technologists, their science and technology will be directed to attempting to ensure the survival of Planet Earth?" (1991:58). Granted these are broad-brush, even rhetorical questions, but the answers shape the type of technology curriculum that will be developed. For instance, in adult life, "cooperative and constructive endeavor" aimed at ensuring "the survival of Planet Earth" must involve dialogue between experts and users. This requires respect for different experiences, a readiness to debate conflicting perspectives and values, and an acceptance of responsibility for the community as a whole and its wider interactive relationships. People are totally unprepared for such participation in decision making if their education gave them no experience of probing the social, environmental, moral, and spiritual issues associated with technological products and processes, and of making carefully considered value judgments.

In recent years, technology education has become an important part of general education in many countries. "Well beyond what might be achieved through traditional technical courses.... [there is] wide recognition that enabling pupils to make sense of technology should be one of the major priorities of the curriculum of the future" (Barnett 1994:52). The World Council of Associations for Technology Education (WOCATE) includes in its mission statement the intention to focus international efforts toward "recognition of the diverse and lifelong nature of Technology Education and the importance of the complex interactions between technological, social, and natural environments" (1993:10). Its founding conference also declared:

> The quality of life afforded by a society is directly related to the extent to which its peoples understand, effectively use, and develop technologies.

> Technology education develops critical survival skills for citizens in a society dominated by change (:14).

How such declarations translate into a technology curriculum is itself the result of complex interactions between economic, political, social, and environmental concerns, and ultimately the worldviews of curriculum developers. "Traditionally, technology courses have concentrated on technique, on questions of *how*, but goals of technological literacy require serious consideration of purposes and outcomes—questions of *why*, and *with what result*" (Barnett 1994:53). As a follow-up to the World Conference on Education for All in 1990, UNESCO organized a large-scale project "2000+: Scientific and Technological Literacy for All," which addressed the question "What kinds of educational provisions and teaching are needed to ensure scientific and technological literacy for all, which in one extreme set of circumstances may be a requirement for survival, and in another for national economic development which does not jeopardise environmental quality?" (Layton 1993b:16). One of the emerging issues was the social shaping of school technology. Taking the case of the technology curriculum in England, David Layton identified a number of stakeholders:

- *Economic functionalists* who insist that school technology should lay the foundations of knowledge and skills for future training, especially in relation to intermediate vocational qualifications;

- *Professional technologists* who think that school technology should be characterized by rigour, working to industrial standards of quality, and the acquisition of knowledge in mainstream engineering areas;

- *Sustainable developers* who emphasize that school technology should empower people with the knowledge, skills, and values to undertake and control technological developments which achieve an acceptable quality of life not only for us, but for succeeding generations, North and South;

- *Women* who urge that school technology should enable girls to define technological challenges, and respond to them, on their own terms, so countering gender biases incorporated in present-day representations of technology;

- *Liberal educators* who are concerned that school technology should initiate children into the unique cognitive mode of technology and help them to construct and control this symbolic world (:18).

The outcome of the debate among these value positions affects the skills, knowledge, perceptions, and attitudes that are actually taught and encouraged in schools. It affects, for example, the breadth of understanding of what constitutes "technological capability," the messages about technology conveyed in the attitudes of the teachers, the choice of products made or evaluated, the constraints that are taken into account, the criteria that are used for evaluation, the extent to which fitness *of* purpose is considered as well as fitness *for* purpose. It is into this debate that Christians can contribute the priorities, the voice and the structure that have emerged out of the examination of technology from a biblical perspective.

### Educating for Responsibility

One focus of the debate is the responsibilities that are to be taught and learned, bearing in mind that "technology curricula need to be *realistic* in reflecting the real world of technological activity, and *feasible* in terms of pupil characteristics and the nature of the school context" (Medway 1993:29). Barnett gives an example:

If the responsibility of the designer is to be taught, what degree of "realism" should be striven for? In the real world of technology, to whom and for what is the designer responsible?—to mankind in general for the future of the planet, or to a line manager for the efficiency of a sub-system meeting the specific technical requirements of a tightly-drawn design brief? As a rule, the autonomy and discretion of designers is strictly limited.... Should the technology curriculum mirror the circumscribed reality of designer-as-technician or attempt to pre-figure alternative, value-sensitive practices in which wider responsibilities are acknowledged? (1994:56).

Is realism to be equated with "industrial design activity that is not driven by necessity as much as commercial opportunity" (Bozeat 1996) or with an assessment of the pressing needs of people and the natural environment? A group of eight Quaker schools in England felt that they were faced with a foregone conclusion in favor of the former by draft proposals for assessment criteria for public examinations in technology:

The proposals would not encourage any pupil to take the needs of the poor seriously, let alone recognize the impressive technical achievements of the third world. There would be no incentive to consider such issues as the supply of fresh water or the unnecessary promotion of baby food mixes in developing countries. Intermediate or appropriate technology was not mentioned. Nor were alternative modes of production. The document seemed to take for granted a whole bundle of assumptions concerning the nature and purpose of design and technological activity... that it should be high tech, profit orientated, capitalist in inspiration (Pitt 1991:34).

It is in keeping with the biblical perspective on technology that one of those schools, the Mount School in York, then developed, and put into practice through the projects undertaken by the pupils, a design and technology curriculum aimed at "equipping pupils to become active collaborators in the creation of a more peaceful, just, and sustainable society" (:34). Their stated aims list widely recognized facets of technological capability—identifying areas of human need, generating design proposals, making artifacts or systems, and appraising processes and outcomes of technological activity— but add the explicit intention of enabling and encouraging the pupils:

- to deepen their concern for the poor and those at the margins of society (both locally and internationally);

- to deepen their awareness of the need to look after the earth's resources and ecosystem;

- to challenge racial and gender stereotyping;

- to develop respect for others, and the skills necessary to work in groups (including the ability to be self-critical and to accept criticism from others) (:35).

There is an underlying assumption here that education for responsible participation in a rapidly changing technological world depends not so much on the "realism" of exact replication of industrial techniques and constraints, but on developing the skills needed to explore the full human and environmental context of any project and to reflect critically on its purpose and outcome. The need is not for training in order to be a compliant operator in production for a consumer market, but for education that gives a person confidence to pay careful and compassionate attention to those who might be implicated, to weigh responsibly any conflict of interests, and to make explicit the basis on which they are making the necessary value judgments. The priority is not learning a fixed body of knowledge and skills, but learning how to use that knowledge and those skills to respond to the needs of the community with sensitivity, imagination, and courage.

## Designing for Quality

The current National Curriculum in England and Wales states: "Pupils should be taught to develop their design and technology capability through combining their Designing and Making skills with Knowledge and understanding in order to design and make products" (DE 1995:2). One aspect of the "knowledge and understanding" is the ability to identify and use criteria that help the pupils judge the quality of a product, including:

(a) how far it meets a clear need;

(b) its fitness for purpose;

(c) whether it is an appropriate use of resources;

(d) its impact beyond the purpose for which it was designed (:9).

This invites an understanding of quality that includes far more than appearance and function. Espousing technical and aesthetic values is not enough; judgment of quality requires exploration of the product's implications and impact. Such a definition opens up the possibility of encouraging pupils to use criteria such as those drawn up by the Mount School:

1. How does it (both process and product) serve to satisfy the real needs of those at the bottom of society, immediately and in the long term, locally and globally?

2. What is the ecological impact?

3. Is it enabling in its *process* as well as its product? Or are people alienated, bored, stupefied?

4. Does it (both process and product) serve to hide or highlight relationships of domination and oppression within society? In particular, does it challenge sexist and consumerist assumptions?

5. How does it allow for or encourage participation among consumers and others affected?

6. Is it durable and easily reparable?

7. Is it comprehensible to the nonspecialist?

8. Is it reversible or modifiable if seen to be in need of improvement?

9. Is it necessary at all? (Pitt 1991:35).

The last criterion forces consideration not just of fitness *for* purpose, but of fitness *of* the purpose. This in turn requires a technology education that allows reflection on fundamental beliefs and values:

> Antipersonnel mines score highly on fitness for purpose and affordability, but their effect on environment and quality of life is (intentionally) disastrous. Should they therefore be classed as good or poor quality products?

> It is only within a framework which highlights questions of value that the complex and potentially contradictory nature of the notion of a "quality product" can be explored. An approach which is value-purblind will seek to ignore these contradictions, but once words such as "quality" are deployed with the intention that they should mean something more than "well-crafted," then it is difficult to force the genie of values back into the bottle of "fitness for purpose" (Barnett 1994:57).

Taking military technology as an acute case of dissociating quality of design from fitness of the purpose, Barnett faces the question as to whether technology education should realistically prepare young people for "the unacknowledged contract of employment that involves the sale of conscience along with labor":

> A truthful reflection of the real world of technology would acknowledge that many people, whether or not by unfettered choice, get their livings in the process of devising and fashioning engines of death, and that much money, material, and ingenuity is thereby expended. An idealistic, forward-looking curriculum, *critically* aware of what is, and concerned with what *ought* to be, might wish to promote the view that it

should neither be, nor seem, "normal" for this to be the case (:59).

## Technology *is* the Context

"Social purposes are lived out *through* technology—technology embodies the purposes and constitutes our lives" (Olson 1993:2). It is therefore not enough to ensure that a technological activity or product is examined in its context, exposing the human and environmental implications and even asking questions about its purpose: it has to be acknowledged that technologies *are* the context. Technology is itself shaping the value judgments we are making about it. As pointed out earlier, this is the power technology exercises over us. Living *in* and acting *on* the world cannot be separated. If by default or lack of more fundamental sources of inspiration and commitment we let the technological environment dominate our experience, then technology will itself become the guiding force for action.

It is for this reason above all that "there is a need to bring values up into the light of day in the teaching and learning of design and technology; to categorize them and make them the subject of deliberation and critical reflection between pupils and between pupils and teachers" (Layton 1992:53). It is also the reason why Layton includes in his list of functional competencies to be taught through the technology curriculum that of "technological evaluation or *critic competence*":

> The ability to judge the worth of a technological development in the light of personal values and to step outside the "mental set" to evaluate what it is doing to us (e.g., it might be encouraging a view of social problems in terms of a succession of "technological fixes" rather than more fundamental considerations) (Layton 1993a:61).

*Critic competence* is the kingpin of technology education. Without it, there is a slide into trivialization, giving young people skills but no confidence in putting those skills to worthwhile and responsible use, and no awareness of the enticing but shallow foundations that technology itself is building into "the house in which we all live."

## Educating the Educators

If technology education is indeed to help young people develop skills of critical reflection on "what is" and on "what ought to be," and if it is to prepare them for effective participation in and for communities that are heavily influenced by technology, it will depend above all on the attitude and approach of teachers who have themselves first reflected on the *"why,* and *with what result."* If critic competence is to be taught, it must first be learned.

This is not to deny the importance of dealing with the technical questions of *how.* A major focus in the training of technology teachers must be specialist knowledge and skills, both those generic to all technological activity (e.g., problem-solving procedures, feedback mechanisms) and those that are specific to a particular branch of technology such as mechanical engineering, textiles, electronics, food technology, graphics, biotechnology. There must also be a focus on the pedagogy, on how teachers can convey their skills, knowledge, understanding, and enthusiasm in a way that releases and develops their pupils' capability, creativity, and ability to work constructively with others. But technology teachers have to be weaned away from the easy route of isolating products from the complexities of their context, relying on specialist expertise and teaching as if technology is value-free. They "need encouragement to include reflection on moral values, and social relations reified in technical objects" (Hansen and Olson 1993:7). They also have to acknowledge that "technical ways of knowing and acting do not provide the tools for analyzing the moral value of technical systems" (Olson 1993:2). Along with all other teachers, they will need to ground their teaching in an honest reflection on their own beliefs and convictions and be ready to learn how "to live on the edge and to deal with uncertainties" (Riggs 1996:8):

> "Good" teacher education necessarily implies enabling future teachers to think about and justify what they

will be doing as teachers in terms of fundamental beliefs about humans, society, nature, knowledge, and ethics. This is essential if they are to be autonomous in the sense of being able to take responsibility for their actions as teachers (Bearlin 1987:2).

In the United Kingdom there have been a number of initiatives to "ensure that adequate consideration is given to value judgments in design and technology and the beliefs that underpin the value judgments; and to promote appropriate classroom strategies for this" (DATA 1997:2). These initiatives share Barnett's conclusion:

> If we accept the "must do better (or else)" verdict on the human technological record, then technology education needs a significant focus on what might be. The role of *critique*, i.e., critical analysis with a view to informing better practice, must be acknowledged.... The key question, however, in view of all the possibilities which [new technologies] may open up, is "what is worth doing?" Many things are *possible*, but what is *worthwhile*? Who shall decide what is worthwhile, and on what criteria? (Barnett 1994:62).

Glenda Prime, of the faculty of education of the University of the West Indies, offered an approach to this key question at the time of the founding of WOCATE:

> It is probably true that the Caribbean and other "developing" countries have a unique contribution to make to world thinking about technology education. For in the majority world, where unemployment and underemployment are rife, where large numbers of people exist on subsistence farming, and where capital for large scale investment is scarce, we will be forced to see technology education from an entirely different perspective from the one which is seen in industrialized nations. We will have to strip it bare of its "high-tech" trappings and see its true role as the empowerment of all our people to improve their own

lives, through self-reliance and interdependence and through the enhancement of social and international relationships—a role that is perhaps equally applicable to all nations but is often under-emphasized where survival needs are not so glaring. The Caribbean contribution can be the placing of this aspect of technology education in center stage (1993:supplement).

Prime here judges "worthwhile" by the criteria of social justice, empowerment, interdependence, and the enhancement of relationships. One cannot overestimate, however, the changes of heart that are needed if these are to become the dominant emphases! Much more prevalent is the "impulse to go on inventing, developing, and producing regardless of society's needs" (Pacey 1983:171). Furthermore, as already noted, technology teachers often find it difficult to acknowledge that they are handling more than a purely technical subject, one in which "the most fundamental choices are between attitudes in mind" (:169); nor do they find it easy to open up issues that might have life-changing consequences. But if sights are to be set on "justice, peace, and the integrity of creation" (to use the motto launched in 1983 by the Sixth Assembly of the World Council of Churches), a technology education is needed that will stimulate, rather than stifle, thoughtful debates on priorities, on what ought to be developed and for what purpose—an education that opens hearts and minds to expectations and commitments that are ultimately of far greater significance than those generated from within technology itself.

# 10

# A Concluding Invitation

But the harvest of the Spirit is love, joy, peace, patience, kindness, goodness, fidelity, gentleness, and self-control. Against such things there is no law. Those who belong to Christ Jesus have crucified the old nature with its passions and desires. If the Spirit is the source of our life, let the Spirit also direct its course (Gal. 5:22–25).

This book has been written in the belief that Christians have a contribution to make to the debates on purpose and priorities; that they have significant expectations and commitments that they can share with colleagues and that will inform their value judgments. But this presupposes that members of the Christian community are encouraged to dig deep into the biblical witness and into their own living faith in order to relate them to the daily experience of living in a technological society. There is here an implied question to Christian leaders and educators as to how they effectively stimulate critical reflection on the demands and implications of what is now a global culture. How, for instance, can Christians be helped to grasp the significance of the world as gift—created, redeemed, and sustained by a compassionate and loving God—when prevalent attitudes look no further than appropriating the world for human "value-added" activity? What shared experiences could best illuminate, in the reality of today's consumer society, the way and mind of Jesus? How indeed can the Christian community become a truly participatory, covenant community, living by grace and forgiveness, and witnessing to an alternative way of enframing and using technological skills?

This is an agenda that challenges the content and the process of Christian education programs (including sermons!). The task is urgent because, although none of us can avoid living in the technological house or the choices it presents, the relevant connections to Christian insights are often not made. So those who are members of the Body of Christ, who are building on the foundation of gratitude, praise, and service to the God made known in Jesus, need to help each other discern the attitudes of mind and heart that reflect his love and openness. Only by growing into this way of being and acting can the web of technological decision making become part of the movement toward the *shalom* of Christ's kingdom.

I have tried in this book to make a contribution to that process of discerning. *Shalom* will become a reality as:

- The experience of marginalized people on the underside of technology is recognized as a key source of wisdom for reshaping it;

- Profound respect is shown for nature's life-sustaining processes;

- Every effort is made to remove "blinkers" and to bring "externalities" into the picture;

- Addressing needs is given priority over creating wants;

- Personal responsibilities are shouldered, not abdicated, for the products of technology;

- Technologies are aimed at empowering others rather than controlling them;

- Electronic communication is not allowed to displace the trust and understanding nurtured in face-to-face relationships, nor to weaken responsibility for immediate neighbors;

- The fruits of incessant technological change are measured against the durable harvest of the Spirit (Gal. 5:22).

These all emphasize the importance of encompassing the whole of a situation, so that technical expertise is held together with a mature understanding of how persons, societies, and nature interrelate. This denies a "technical fix" approach that puts complete faith in a technological solution, which ignores both other more appropriate responses (invest in "loving your enemy" rather than building more nuclear warheads) and the reality of human fallibility and sinfulness (the technologist is just as likely as anyone else to fall prey to greed, hunger for power, and a failure in relationships). The focus on wholeness also integrates the concern for social justice with that for eco-justice, the "experts" with the "users," the masculine with the feminine. Above all, wholeness for Christians involves an openness to the Spirit in all the value judgments and decisions made on our pilgrimages as disciples of Jesus within a technological culture. May we pray with St. Paul: "If the Spirit is the source of our life, let the Spirit also direct its course" (Gal. 5:25).

# Notes

1. Schools in England and Wales have a statutory duty to promote "pupils' spiritual, moral, social, and cultural" development. Partly to clarify how schools might be supported in this task, the School Curriculum and Assessment Authority set up a National Forum for Values in Education and the Community, and in 1996 initiated a project to produce guidance material for schools. This includes highlighting how each subject area, including Design and Technology, contributes to the spiritual, moral, social, and cultural development of pupils.

2. Originally prompted in 1987 by an education group within the British Council of Churches' program "The Gospel and Our Culture," there has grown up an informal network of technology educators, VALIDATE (Values in Design and Technology Education), "to promote discussion of values as an essential dimension of Design and Technology education at all ages" (DATA 1997). It is now a broad-based network linked to professional technology teachers' associations. It has been responsible for a booklet published by the Department for Education and Employment in 1995, *Looking at Values Through Products and Applications*, and for the DATA Guidance Notes in 1997. The Web site is www.data.org.uk/values.

Other organizations that have produced excellent material for in-service teacher education and classroom strategies include the Birmingham Development Education Centre, 998 Bristol Road, Birmingham B29 6LE, U.K.; and Intermediate Technology (Education Department), The Schumacher Centre for Technology and Development, Bourton Hall, Bourton-on-Dunsmore, Rugby, Warwickshire CV23 9QZ, U.K.

# References Cited

Barbour, Ian. 1992. *Ethics in An Age of Technology*. London: SCM Press.

Barnett, Michael. 1994. Designing the future? Technology, Values, and Choice. *International Journal of Technology and Design Education* 4:1:51–63.

Bearlin, Margareet L. 1987. Feminist Critiques of Science: Implications for Teacher Education. Paper presented at GASAT 4 Conference. Gender and Science and Technology Association, c/o Dr J. Harding, 6, Ullswater Grove, Alresford, Hants SO24 9NP, UK.

Borgmann, Albert. 1984. *Technology and the Character of Contemporary Life: A Philosophical Inquiry*. Chicago: University of Chicago Press.

Bosch, David. 1995. *Believing in the Future*. Valley Forge, Pa.: Trinity Press International.

Bozeat, Rupert. 1996. Developing an appreciation of our technological heritage through education and interactive multimedia. Paper presented at JISTEC '96. Jerusalem International Science and Technology Conference 1996.

Brody, Hugh. 1981. *Maps and Dreams*. London: Pelican Books.

CEC (Conference of European Churches) and CCEE (Council of European Bishops' Conferences). 1995. *Peace: Precarious and Precious*. Report on a team visit to churches in Northern Ireland and the Republic of Ireland.

Chapman, Bryan. 1991, The Overselling of Science Education in the Eighties. *School Science Review* 72(260):47–63.

Christie, Michael J. 1991. Aboriginal Science for the Ecologically Sustainable Future. *Australian Science Teachers Journal* 37:1:26–31.

Cobb, Clifford. 1992. Reflections of a Neo-Luddite. *The Human Economy Newsletter* 13:3.

Cobb, John B. 1994. *Sustaining the Common Good*. Cleveland, Ohio: The Pilgrim Press.

Cole-Turner, R. 1993. *New Genesis: Theology and the Genetic Revolution*. London: Westminster Press.

Conway, Ruth. 1992. Review of Borgmann, A. (see above). *British Journal of Religious Education* 14:4.

Crumlin, Rosemary and Anthony Knight. 1991. *Aboriginal Art and Spirituality*. Victoria, Australia: Collins Dove.

Daly, Herman E. 1993. Elements of Environmental Macroeconomics. Reproduced in *Sustainable Growth: A Contradiction in Terms?* Geneva: The Visser't Hooft Endowment Fund for Leadership Development. Available from the World Council of Churches.

DATA Guidance Notes. 1997. *Exploring Value Judgements in Design and Technology.* The Design and Technology Association, Wellesbourne, Warwickshire CV35 9JB, UK.

Davis, John. 1994. Without a Vision the People Perish. *Audenshaw Papers* 154. Oxford: The Hinksey Centre, Westminster College.

DfE (Department for Education). 1995. *Design and Technology in the National Curriculum*. London: HMSO.

DfEE (Department for Education and Employment). 1995. *Looking at Values Through Products and Applications*. London: DfEE.

Dowley, Roger. 1984. *Towards the Recovery of a Lost Bequest*. London: Evangelical Coalition for Urban Mission.

Dyson, Anthony. 1993. *Ethics and the New Reproductive Technologies*. Canterbury: Centre for the Study of Religion and Society, University of Kent.

Eliot, T. S. 1948. Choruses from "The Rock." *Selected Poems*. London: Penguin.

Elliott, Charles. 1988. *Signs of Our Times*. London: Marshall Pickering.

Faith and Politics Group. 1997. *Doing Unto Others: Parity of Esteem in a Contested Space*. Belfast: The Faith and Politics Group, c/o the Corrymeela Community.

Franklin, Ursula. 1985. *Will Women Change Technology or Will Technology Change Women?* Toronto, Ontario: ICREF/CRIAW.

——. 1992. *The Real World of Technology*. Toronto, Ontario: Anansi Press.

Furuya, Keiichi. 1989. Toward the Ethics of Engineering. *World Student Christian Federation Journal*. Issue on *Faith, Science, and Technology*. Geneva: WSCF.

Gosling, David. 1986. Introduction. *Technology from the Underside*. [TUGON VI:1]. Manila: National Council of Churches in the Philippines.

Grant, George. 1986. *Technology and Justice*. Toronto, Ontario: Anansi Press.

Habgood, John. 1980. *A Working Faith*. London: Darton, Longman & Todd.

——. 1994. Where Do Babies Come From? London: *The Independent*, 11 January 1994.

Hansen, Klaus-Henning and John Olson. 1993. Rethinking Technology in Education: An Action Research Approach. Unpublished project proposal. Mathematics, Science, and Technology Education Group, Queens University, Ontario.

Harrison, Mark. 1995. *Visions of Heaven and Hell*. London: Channel 4 Television.

Hynes, H. Patricia, ed. 1989. *Reconstructing Babylon: Essays on Women and Technology*. London: Earthscan Publications.

——. 1994. Gender and the Teaching and Learning of Technology. *Innovations in Science and Technology Education V*. Edited by David Layton. Paris: UNESCO.

Jonas, Hans. 1984. *The Imperative of Responsibility*. Chicago: University of Chicago Press.

Korten, David C. 1996. When Corporations Rule the World. *Human Economy* 15:1.

Larsen, J. K. 1989. How High-Tech Is Changing American Society. *The New Faith-Science Debate*. Edited by John M. Mangum. Geneva: WCC; Minneapolis: Fortress Press.

Layton, David. 1992. Values in Design and Technology. *Make the Future Work. Appropriate Technology: A Teachers' Guide*. Edited by Catherine Budgett-Meakin. Harlow: Longman Group UK for Intermediate Technology.

———. 1993a. *Technology's Challenge to Science Education*. Buckingham, UK; Bristol, Pa.: Open University Press.

———. 1993b. Design and Technology in Schools: A Comparative View. *Design & Technology Teaching* 25(2):16–20.

Lebacqz, Karen. 1987. *Justice in An Unjust World*. Minneapolis: Augsburg Publishing House.

Ledger, Christine. 1989. The Ideology of Science. *World Student Christian Federation Journal*. Issue on *Faith, Science, and Technology*. Geneva: WSCF.

Lochhead, David. 1997. *Shifting Realities*. Geneva: WCC.

Lutzenberger, José. 1996. Development Is a Sham. *New Internationalist* 278:20–22.

Mander, Jerry. 1991. *In the Absence of the Sacred: The Failure of Technology and the Survival of the Indian Nations*. San Francisco: Sierra Club Books.

McDaniel, Jay. 1990. "Where is the Holy Spirit Anyway? Response to a Sceptic Environmentalist." *The Ecumenical Review* 42(2):162–174.

McFadyen, Alistair. 1997. Christians in Public Life: The Theological Challenge. *Changing World, Unchanging Church?* Edited by David Clark. London: Mowbray.

Medway, Peter. 1993. Issues in the Theory and Practice of Technology Education. *School Science and Technology: Some Issues and Perspectives*. Edited by E. W. Jenkins. Leeds, UK: Centre for Studies in Science and Mathematics Education.

Mulgan, Geoff. 1994. Networks for An Open Society. *Demos* Quarterly Issue 4: *Liberation Technology?*

Müller-Fahrenholz, Geiko. 1995. *God's Spirit: Transforming a World in Crisis*. New York: Continuum; Geneva, WCC.

Mumford, Lewis. 1944. *The Condition of Man*. New York: Harcourt, Brace and Company.

Northcott, Michael S. 1996. *The Environment and Christian Ethics*. Cambridge: Cambridge University Press.

Norton-Taylor, Richard. 1996. CIA Turns Green. *The Guardian*, 11 September 1996.

Olson, John. 1993. Technology as Social Context. Unpublished paper for workshop, Exploring the Relationship of Science, Technology, and Society in Education. IPN, Kiel.

Pacey, Arnold. 1983. *The Culture of Technology*. Cambridge: Massachusetts Institute of Technology Press.

Pacey, Arnold. 1992. *The Maze of Ingenuity*. 2nd Edition. Cambridge: Massachusetts Institute of Technology Press.

Patel, Kam. 1993. Erring on the Side of You-Manity. *The Guardian*, 13 August 1993.

Pitt, James. 1991. Design and Technology and Social Responsibility. *Design & Technology Teaching* 24(1):34–36.

Postel, Sandra. 1996. Sharing the Rivers. *People and the Planet* 15(3):6–9.

Postman, Neil. 1993. *Technopoly: The Surrender of Culture to Technology*. New York: Vintage Books.

POSTnote 56. January 1995. London: Parliamentary Office of Science and Technology, House of Commons.

Pursell, Carroll. 1994. *White Heat*. London: BBC.

Rasmussen, Larry L. 1996. *Earth Community, Earth Ethics*. Geneva: WCC.

Riggs, Anne. 1996. Beliefs, Values, Science, and Technology Education. Paper given at Morals for the Millennium Conference, University College of St. Martin, Lancaster, UK.

Robinson, John A. T. 1983. The Christian Dimension of the Energy Problem. Edited Conference Papers. London: Commission for International Justice and Peace.

Sachs, Wolfgang. 1989. Technology as a Trojan Horse. *On the Archaeology of the Development Idea*. State College, Pa.: Pennsylvania State University.

Shenk, Wilbert R. 1995. *Write the Vision*. Valley Forge, Pa.: Trinity Press International.

Slouka, Mark. 1996. *War of the Worlds: Cyberspace and the High-Tech Assault on Reality*. New York: Basic Books, 1995; London: Abacus, 1996.

Staudenmaier, John M. 1987. *Advent for Capitalists: Grief, Joy, and Gender in Contemporary Society*. Nash Lecture, Campion College, University of Regina, Saskatchewan, Canada.

Tomlinson, J. 1990. *New Visions for Old*. Times Educational Supplement, 5 January1990.

Turner, Eva. 1998. Women into Computing: What Is Being Done to Promote It! GASAT 1998 European Conference paper, available from <e.turner@mdx.ac.uk>.

van den Heuvel, Albert. 1997. "Pray—and Do Justice!" *Link*. European Newsletter of the World Association for Christian Communication 3:8.

Waks, Leonard J. 1994. Value Judgment and Social Action in Technology Studies. *International Journal of Technology and Design Education* 4:1:35–47.

Waters, Brent. 1990. Pilgrims and Progress: Technology and Christian Ethics. *Bulletin of the Center for Theology and the Natural Sciences* 10:4.

Weber, Hans-Ruedi. 1981. *Experiments with Bible Study*. Geneva: WCC.

Williams, Rowan. 1995. *The Kingdom Is Theirs*. London: Christian Socialist Movement .

Wink, Walter. 1984. *Naming the Powers*. Minneapolis: Fortress Press.

——. 1986. *Unmasking the Powers*. Philadelphia: Fortress Press.

——. 1992. *Engaging the Powers*. Minneapolis: Fortress Press.

Winner, Langdon. 1986. *The Whale and the Reactor*. Chicago: University of Chicago Press.

———. 1992. Citizen Virtues in a Technological Order. *Inquiry* 35(3–4):46–68. Also published in *Applied Ethics: A Reader*. Edited by E. R. Winkler and J. R. Coombs. 1993. Oxford: Blackwell.

WOCATE (World Council of Associations for Technology Education). 1993. *Newsletter* 1:1.

World Council of Churches. 1991. *Signs of the Spirit: Official Report of the Seventh Assembly*. Edited by Michael Kinnamon. Geneva: WCC.

Woudhuysen, James. 1994. Before We Rush to Declare a New Era. *Demos* Quarterly Issue 4: *Liberation Technology?*